Shark Tank India

Shark Tank India

Start-up Fundas from the Sharks and Participants

Shark Tank India

with

Prerna Lidhoo

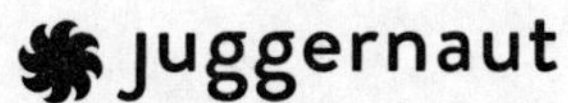

JUGGERNAUT BOOKS
C-I-128, First Floor, Sangam Vihar, Near Holi Chowk,
New Delhi 110 080, India

First published by Juggernaut Books 2023

10 9 8 7 6 5 4 3 2

P-ISBN: 9789353451615
E-ISBN: 9789353451622

Typeset in Adobe Caslon Pro by R. Ajith Kumar, Noida

Printed at Thomson Press India Ltd

To India's start-up founders –
past, present, future

Contents

Introduction

So you want to start a start-up?

Do you have an idea for a business? Are you willing to take big risks to make it big? Maybe you want to take part in the next season of *Shark Tank India*? Then you're at the right place.

Welcome to *Shark Tank India: Start-up Fundas from the Sharks and Participants*. In this book, India's most inspiring entrepreneurs, the six amazing Sharks of *Shark Tank India* – Namita, Peyush, Aman, Anupam, Amit and Vineeta – give you their hacks, all their fundas and a ton of stories, which will help you turn your start-up dreams into reality.

In extensive interviews, they describe their lives and business backgrounds. They outline the lessons they have learnt while running their businesses. They also explain what they think an entrepreneur needs to cultivate in terms of mindsets and qualities.

Some qualities such as optimism, empathy, flexibility, ability to absorb advice, passion about the business and so on, do pop up again and again, in every Shark's opinions. But there's obviously a difference in their thinking processes. We know this because only three pitches in the first season and four in the second season received a joint offer by all the Sharks and most pitches that received offers at all, received offers from three Sharks or even fewer. Some pitches received an offer from only one Shark.

We'll return to this subject later, in the chapter, 'Lessons from *Shark Tank India*', where we'll look at some of the pitches that ended up as successful businesses post the show, and discover their learnings as rookie start-ups. In the conclusion, we'll also detail some of the things that could help you get through the qualifier process, make a pitch and hopefully, win an offer.

Start-ups are a slog

Being an entrepreneur is not all about glamour and jazzy presentations. Running a business is a difficult process and presents quite a few challenges. Running a start-up is a real time-sink – forget about spending extended time with family, going on holidays and indulging in hobbies. There are enormous stresses and it can be an emotional roller coaster since there will be setbacks and failures.

It might not be your cup of tea – Shark Aman Gupta said that his wife tried to set up a business and quit within months because she couldn't handle the stress. Vineeta Singh says she cries when she's feeling frustrated; Namita Thapar says she does regular meditation to try and maintain her calm.

Ganesh Balakrishnan of Flatheads, made a pitch, got an offer and decided to shut down his business anyway because he felt he needed time to reset his mental balance. If you realize that entrepreneurship is not the journey you wish to make, well, this book might save you some heartache. There's no shame in that.

The step-by-step guide to setting up

If on the other hand, you decide you want to launch a start-up, read the book, absorb the learnings and lessons the Sharks offer, and make them your own. But before you leap in, let's spell out the steps by which you begin to set up your business.

Step 1: The business idea

This is key and many of the chapters in this book will help you think about what makes a winning idea. Each of the Sharks and the competitors came to their businesses in different ways – but there was always some big-picture thinking connected to it. Be it Vineeta Singh's vision of India's growing number of empowered women, or Jimmy Shah (the mom is Jimmy!) discovering there wasn't a range of ice creams for diabetics like herself. The big picture was also backed up by research – the most successful founders thought about the market size, what need the product addressed and who their competitors were.

HOW TO MAKE A BUSINESS PLAN

You should make a business plan (BP) to flesh out your idea. This plan helps you clarify your strategy, identify resources and possible roadblocks, identify the competition, work out the financials and so on. A coherent business plan is also vital if you're trying to raise funding.

When you write a business plan, you're second-guessing your own ideas and checking them to see if they work in practice. You're also looking to attract hard-nosed investors who will back you with their resources.

Keep it short, keep it simple. Make sure you can handle deeper questions, which any investor who reads the plan and likes it, will ask.

Here's one way to write a BP:

Start with a **Mission Statement:** This should be simple, succinct and ambitious. 'Make diabetic-friendly ice-cream' or 'Become the online resource for somebody who wants to buy a personal vehicle.'

Write an **Executive Summary:** This will describe the following sections in a few sentences. Assume that potential investors are busy and they might not bother to read the rest of the document if they don't like the Summary. Keep this to one page ideally.

Product/ Service Description: Describe your product or service. Why do you think there's a market for this? Explain this in some detail.

Marketing and Competition Analysis: How do you intend to market your product/service? Who are your competitors or potential competitors? Why do you think you have an edge or think you can develop an edge? Do you need to build a brand? How will you do this? What is your distribution network going to be? What's your planned operational structure? The investor will judge you on the basis of the research that goes into this.

Financials and Other Resources: Work out what you need in the way of resources and funding. Work out what you think you can make in terms of revenues, market share and profits. How fast can you scale and how much can you scale? Are you looking for high profits or fast growth or a mix of both? There will be both hard numbers and also guesstimates here. Those have to look realistic.

Bios: Who are you? How many of you are there? What are your skills and experience? How many people do you intend to hire and with what skills? Do you have mentors?

Be aware that a lot of investors will just read the Executive Summary, and anybody who is interested enough to want more information will grill you personally. So write a short plan, focus on the summary, and get somebody who's a friend to ask the awkward questions and help you research and rehearse the answers.

Step 2: Early stage of setting up

Most start-ups begin small to see if their proposition works. Their pilot is usually funded by themselves, friends and family. Aman set up boAt with his savings – which is the common way to begin. As you launch your business with baby steps, you will be looking for proof of concept – also called **a product-market fit, it means the response to your business that shows that your starting proposition works.** Post that, you will need more funds to scale your idea. Most people move to the next stage and look for proper fundraising once they can demonstrate product-market fit.

PRODUCT-MARKET FIT

Here's a typical process to find your product-market fit:

Define your target market: Identify the specific group of customers that your product or service is intended for. The more clearly you can define your target market, the easier it will be to assess whether your product meets their needs.

Gather customer feedback: Ask customers for their thoughts on your product or service. What do they like about it? What do they wish was different? This feedback can be valuable in helping you identify areas where your product could be improved.

Research your competition: Look at the products or services that your competitors are offering and compare them to your own. What are the unique selling points of your product? How does it compare to the competition in terms of price, quality and features?

Analyse your sales and growth: Look at your sales and growth data to see how well your product is doing in the market. If you're experiencing strong growth and high levels of customer satisfaction, it's a good sign that you've found a good product-market fit.

In the first, early phase, however, you must do a few practical things – think of a name register the business with the help of a chartered accountant (CA), create a shareholders' agreement and issue shares, and research how you will make the product.

Registration will require your CA to get you a digital security certificate (DSC) and a director identification number (DIN), as well as create an account on the MCA portal. You may be able to do this yourself as well.

WHAT IS THE MCA?

MCA is the **Ministry of Corporate Affairs website** and is also known as the MCA portal. This portal helps facilitate many services for companies and LLPs (limited liability partnerships), starting from incorporation to closure. They can be found at www.mca.gov.in.

You may also spend some funds designing the product and your logo. You may already have a co-founder with you by this time, but mostly likely you won't have the funds to hire too many people and you'll do a lot of multitasking. Husband and wife Ravi and Anuja Kabra, who set up Skippi popsicles, worked day and night handling almost every part of their business in the early days, and they weren't the only ones.

Here is a checklist to starting a business:

- Create a business plan.
- Research how to make the product and also do market research around your proposition.
- Come up with a business name and check with the MCA. If you have a name that's close to an existing business in the same industry, the name will be rejected.
- Incorporate your business either as a LTD or LLP. A CA or lawyer can advise and help you through the registration stage.
- Apply for trademarks in two to three categories.
- Buy a domain name.
- Figure what your seed round will be. You will have to calculate what your financial needs are and also build in time for a proper fundraise. E.g., X months to create and take product to market, Y months to see how the business fares, Z months to fundraise. Think about where your funds will come from – is this from your own savings, family and friends, or an early angel investor?
- Issue shares (and you will also have to decide how many shares to issue).
- Create a shareholder agreement.

Step 3: Funding and valuations

Start-ups can seek investment at different stages of development and there's no set rule as to when they're ripe for external investments. Some start-ups may seek investment from the very beginning to help fund development of their product or service and simply get the business off the ground. Others may wait until they have a proven track record and are actually generating revenue before seeking investment to help them scale and grow.

So let's imagine the entrepreneur (also called the promoter or founder, or co-founders if there are two or more) raises an initial investment. The investors at this stage are often called 'angels' – this is a term borrowed from the world of theatre and film.

When you incorporate a company, you divide the ownership up by issuing shares. You could issue 100 shares or 100,000, or 1 crore, shares and you could set a face-value of ₹1 or ₹10. The exact numbers don't matter but turning the ownership, into shares makes it easier to allocate fractional ownership, which will be useful later.

The initial capital raised is called the seed fund. This seed capital is often a relatively small amount – for example, Aman and his co-founder each put in ₹30 lakh to launch their own start-up.

Quite often, this seed capital is raised by the promoters

putting in their own savings and tapping family and friends. The initial investors are allotted stakes according to the capital they subscribe and according to their agreements with the founders.

The investment and stakes may be unevenly distributed. Let's consider a concrete example. Say there are two co-founders of a company, ABC Limited, and they invest ₹30 lakh each. They each keep 45% ownership. They raise another ₹50 lakh from angels, while giving the angels a collective 10% stake. Those angels may be their wives or uncles or any friends who invest in ABC. So, the company now has ₹1.10 crore to invest.

Shark Tank India operates at the angel investor stage. The Sharks bargain with the founders who make pitches. The Sharks make offers to invest a certain amount and bargain for a stake in lieu of the capital they offer.

This angel stage is also where the concept of valuation first arises. Let's say a Shark offers ₹1 crore for a 10% stake to ABC, and this offer is accepted and the founders each turn over 5% of their stake to the Shark. Now the entire company is valued at ₹10 crore (10% = ₹1 crore, 100% = ₹10 crore) . The founders now hold 40% each – so, their stakes are each worth ₹4 crore. ABC also now has ₹2.1 crore to invest in developing the business.

There are multiple further stages of possible funding:

Series A funding: A Series A funding is the first round of institutional investment a start-up raises. This cash will generally come from a venture capital (VC) firm or from a private equity (PE) firm. Both VCs and PE investors can get involved from this stage onwards. The difference between the two categories of investors is largely about size of investment. VCs tend to invest smaller amounts at an earlier stage. PE firms tend to invest more at a later stage. But there are no hard and fast rules.

Again, the concept of valuation arises. Let's say our company, ABC, raises ₹20 crore in Series A capital, with each co-founder selling another 5% stake. Now we're seeing a valuation of ₹200 crore for ABC. The founders have each diluted their stakes down 35%, and this 70% stake is worth ₹140 crore.

Series B funding: Series B funding is a second round of institutional investment that a start-up raises. Again, this is used to further accelerate growth and expansion of the business. The valuation changes again, depending on what stake is sold for what amount.

Let's say, ABC receives Series B funding of ₹35 crore for 10% stake. The valuation has risen again to ₹350 crore, with our co-founders now each holding stakes of 30% ownership, which is valued at ₹105 crore.

Series C funding: Series C funding is a third round of institutional investment a start-up raises. It is typically used to further scale the business and to prepare angels and PEs and VCs for a potential exit, such as through an initial public offering (IPO), or through acquisition.

Again, valuations will change. Let's say ABC raises ₹100 crore for another 10% stake dilution – ABC is now valued at ₹1,000 crore. The co-founders still hold 25% stake each. Their stakes are each worth ₹250 crore.

Notice how the valuation of ABC has dramatically increased at every stage and how ABC, which had raised 'only' ₹157.1 crore, is now valued at ₹1,000 crore. This is what can happen when there's a good business plan, validated by healthy revenue streams. This process then works as an excellent recipe for wealth creation.

Other funding options

Assume ABC becomes quite successful. The company plans to scale up further to increase capacity and to hire more people, etc.

It's estimated ABC needs another ₹1,000 crore to fund the next stage of expansion. Where does it find this money?

There are several options:

1. ABC has made, say, ₹5 crore in profits over the last few years, so a little of the requirement can be funded through profits. This is known as funding via **internal accruals.**
2. The company may raise more money from VCs.
3. The company can seek to get a bank loan. This is funding through '**debt.**'
4. **The company can go public with an IPO.**
5. The company can issue bonds, which means that it's raising debt from the public.

Let's say, ABC decides on an IPO. It hires an investment banker. It decides to sell 25% stake to the public and list ABC on the stock exchange. This implies that the valuation would rise from ₹1,000 crore to ₹4,000 crore.

Now, by this stage, the co-founders still own 25% each and there are VCs, angels, etc., who have invested in ABC at various stages. They can all offer a part or all of their stake, cash in some profits. ABC as a corporate entity meanwhile receives the cash it needs to continue growing.

This is a very simplified description of the processes by which a start-up can grow and be funded and create wealth. There's a lot of hard work, a lot of paperwork and a lot of luck that goes into making a business successful enough to reach IPO status.

But this sort of wealth creation does happen. It may seem like magic but it happened 108 times in 2022 – that is, 108 businesses launched IPOs. Entrepreneurs with great business ideas, and a competent management team can hit the jackpot and that dream drives many promoters.

Classic real-world examples of such wealth creation stories would be Infosys, Reliance, Eicher Motors, Titan Industries, and in the international space, one could think of Google, Facebook, Amazon, Tesla, Twitter, AliBaba, etc.

Think of a pyramid. It has a wide base but it tapers as it rises. There's very little room at the top. Success at business is like that. There are thousands of bright, enthusiastic young entrepreneurs founding businesses every year. A few receive funding and grow beyond the mom-and-pop stage. Of those few, even fewer make it to an IPO and stock exchange listing.

Even after crossing the IPO hurdle, businesses have been known to fail and go bankrupt. For every Infosys, there are a hundred software businesses that never made it to an IPO, and there are a dozen that did an IPO but never achieved that level of success.

But that dream of success and wealth multiplication

drives people. Other entrepreneurs may not be that ambitious but they want to be their own boss. Or they simply have a bright idea and they want to run with it.

If you have that fire within you, and you make it to *Shark Tank*, you will go one level up that pyramid.

Enjoy the roller-coaster world you are about to embark on!

1

Vineeta Singh's Secret to Sweet Success

'It's more important to reach the finish line than finish first.'

Do you have an idea for a great business? Well congratulations! That's a great start. But we have bad news. It's just the beginning. You're at the start of a marathon, and you have 42 long, painful, back-breakingly tiring kilometres to go.

Do you have what it takes? Shark Vineeta Singh is a passionate marathon runner who has completed 20 marathons, three ultra-marathons (89 kilometres) and a dozen half-marathons (21 kilometres)! She believes running a marathon and running a company are quite similar.

WHO IS VINEETA SINGH?

Vineeta Singh is the 39-year-old co-founder and CEO of SUGAR Cosmetics. Launched in 2015, it is, today, the fastest-growing premium cosmetics brand in the country. This Indian brand started with just two products – a matte eyeliner and a black kohl pencil. It has since grown to sell a wide-ranging portfolio of all things make-up: foundations, concealers, lipsticks, bronzers, highlighters, etc. The brand's current valuation is $500 million.[1]

In fact, all those marathons have taught her a big lesson that she has used for her work: **'Everyone can't finish first but everybody can reach the finish line, which is why you get a "did not quit" medal if you finish the race. I think that's a core philosophy for me. It's also about understanding that pivoting – a change in direction – is not quitting.'**

Alongside that, she believes her optimism, her ability to handle stress and cope with failure and bounce back have helped make SUGAR the success it is.

LESSON I

Aim for the 'did not quit' medal

All start-up founders will tell you that almost every day, you will be tempted to call it quits. Each day, the fear of failure looms larger than the distant vision of success and it's hard to see the end of the road. But if you have what it takes, you will just keep going. Some of these challenges won't just be in your work life. You will have family who won't see enough of you; friends who have given up on you.

You also need to accept one big, scary thing – that you might lose whatever has been committed to the venture. For Vineeta and her co-founder and husband Kaushik Mukherjee, who both come from middle-class backgrounds, it meant risking their life savings.

Vineeta recalls, 'We plotted these worst-case scenarios, though we know that often it's not as bad as we are imagining and fearing. For me, the worst case would have been losing that last ₹30 lakh I'd set aside in the bank and starting again from square one.' The potential rewards were worth the sacrifices she had to make. 'I never had a fancy lifestyle. I knew I would have to prioritize certain things and not own too many things.'

They eventually decided to go for it. 'Fear kills more dreams than failure ever will. So if there's something that you're really afraid of doing, it's a sign that there's like a big dream hidden behind it. So, just take the plunge, trust your instincts and try it out. What's the worst that can happen? Going back to square one shouldn't be a demotivating factor. There is a massive risk in running a start-up, as chances of failure by default are in the design. **There is no way you should be taking a large risk and not be ready to fail.**'

In addition to the usual challenges that come with running a business, Vineeta has also had to handle the issues that come with being a woman in the workplace.

Women entrepreneurs face even more challenges than their male counterparts. Across India, women are still expected to fulfil traditional roles, such as raising children and managing the household. Starting a business can be seen as going against these expectations, and women may, therefore, face pressure from their families and communities to give up their jobs or find work that's more family-friendly.

There is another harsh reality facing working women in India. They often face discrimination at workplaces, and this can be particularly pronounced for women launching their own businesses. Vineeta often found herself being judged for her looks rather than her intellect, for instance. It was frustrating and demoralizing, especially when her educational pedigree included premier institutions like IIT Madras and IIM Ahmedabad.

Soon after the release of *Shark Tank India* Season 1, Vineeta Singh found herself swamped with memes and trolls attacking her for her appearance. A meme equating her with Raju's mother from the Bollywood film *3 Idiots* went viral.

But instead of feeling sorry for herself, she responded with a hilarious video of herself dressed in a saree like Raju's mother (complete with a black-and-white filter as a nod to the original scene from the movie), sitting in her corner office and citing the rising price of bhindi to turn down a budget request from one of her execs. That little meme worked. It got people laughing about her response rather than the original meme.

There are going to be so many stressful moments, times

when you feel utterly humiliated and when you feel you have no hope.

For Vineeta, rock bottom came at the very beginning of her journey when she turned down a ₹1 crore job offer to start a company that never took off, and then struggled for the next five years. 'Within six months, the most important decision I took turned out to be wrong. I grappled with serious questions like maybe I'm not smart enough to be a founder. I think self-doubt and a lack of self-confidence is probably the worst kind of rock bottom because, you know, there's nothing that anybody else can say that can turn it around for you,' she says.

A few years later, when Fab Bag wasn't scaling and there were salaries to be paid to more than 25 employees, while Vineeta was trying something new in terms of a pivot, she still remembers opening a 'shutdown account', which had some emergency money set aside for the rainy day that would allow them to repay the vendors, pay employees and take care of liabilities. But SUGAR, of course, changed the course of things.

'The first 23 years of my life, I had never seen failure. And then, for the next 10 years, I saw back-to-back failures. So, suddenly from being somebody who thinks she's smart to having all kinds of fundamental doubts, was the hardest phase of my life,' she adds.

Back in 2015, all this was going on when Vineeta was also expecting her first child. 'I never expected I could be so strong. Earlier, I would only dream of whatever I knew I could achieve, and then I would achieve it so I would never feel that I failed. All these years, I really surprised myself. I'm really proud of how far I've come because I know it has not been easy,' she says.

Another person with similar educational qualifications would, perhaps, have decided to walk the safer road. But marathon runners have to slog through about 40 gruelling, painful kilometres before they cross the finish line. Vineeta was prepared to do that, and to just keep running down the road she had chosen. That made all the difference.

LESSON 2

Rethink quitting into pivoting

Now don't think not quitting means gritting your teeth and carrying on in the same painful path you have been going on, wondering if the finishing line will ever come. **The key to never saying die is to be adaptable.** Learning to pivot from your current path is the only way you can get to the finishing line.

Take Vineeta's earlier venture, Fab Bag, for example. This beauty subscription service was started by Vineeta and Kaushik in 2012. It lasted just two-and-a-half years, and it was registering ₹7 crore in revenues when they decided to change direction.

'We realized that it was never going to become a large ₹100-crore company. With every additional consumer we were acquiring, we were losing more money. At that time, there was an option to give up and go back to salaried jobs. I had tried two other start-ups before this, which hadn't worked,' she says.

Vineeta's start-up journey began with a desire to start her own lingerie brand. She had knocked on the doors of several investors but wasn't successful in convincing them to get on board.

But the marathoner didn't give up. It had broken her emotionally to receive those rejections, but she decided to somehow bootstrap a start-up. With almost no money to speak of, she started a service company that would assist other companies to check their employees' backgrounds. She was making as little as ₹10,000 a month, even as scalability and profitability remained key issues.

'It's impossible to become a successful start-up founder if you're not capable of coping with failures and don't know how to handle setbacks and rejections. And if you don't do things that are right by the consumer, then, in the long term, it comes in the way of creating large businesses,' she says.

Every single time, she grappled with two key questions:

Is it worth it?

Am I built to be a founder?

But resilience is at the core of every marathoner. 'So, we took a call that we need to pivot, and that's when we started working on what eventually became SUGAR,' she adds. 'No matter how hard the setback or the failure, just showing up the next day and doing things over and over again makes all the difference.'

Her journey of becoming a Shark from a floundering founder hasn't been an easy one.

> 'Failure sucks! The first big humiliation of my life was when I stood for student union elections in IIM A and received the sum total of seven votes (including my own) from a class of 280 students. I wanted to die and I hid under my desk. Nowadays, after surviving 100 rejections from investors, I just hide my face under a pillow. If you're an entrepreneur, you learn to deal with failure and humiliation, and you learn that eventually, failures lead to wins!'

WHAT DOES PIVOTING MEAN?

Pivoting involves changing the direction of a business in response to changing market conditions or new insights. It can mean changes to the product or service, the target market, the business model or any other aspect of the business.

You should consider pivoting when you are not achieving your desired goals or when it becomes clear that the current business model is not sustainable.

There are a few key signs a company may need to pivot.

1. It is not achieving its desired growth or financial performance: If a company is not meeting its financial or growth targets, it may need to pivot to a new business model or target market in order to become more successful.
2. The market is changing: If the market or industry is changing rapidly, the company may need to pivot in order to stay relevant.
3. It is not able to meet customer needs: If a company is not meeting the needs of its customers, it may need to pivot in order to better serve its target market.
4. It is not able to scale: If a company is unable to scale its business, it may need to pivot in order to find a business model that allows for growth.

LESSON 3

How to make that perfect pivot

According to Vineeta, 90% of the key to success is not giving up, and the rest is knowing when to pivot. Above all, **if your vision is clear and remains constant, and the timing works, a pivot will work. So when you are thinking about making a pivot in your business, ask yourself, why am I doing what I am doing? What do I believe in? What is my business about?**

'I tried multiple times to pivot my business to where I thought the opportunity lay. The reason we were able to pivot from Fab Bag (her first venture into cosmetics) to SUGAR was because we had this fundamental belief that young women are taking control of their lives,' she says.

As the literacy rate of Indian women rises above 70%[2] (across the globe, the average female literacy rate is around 79%[3]), more young women will step into the workforce and they will achieve the financial freedom to spend on products that help build their self-confidence.

This was the basic thesis that led Vineeta and Kaushik to bet on SUGAR as a brand that will be at the forefront of this fundamental change in India's female population's buying power and behaviour. 'When we started Fab Bag, we had a belief that we wanted to be this consumer's best friend. That belief didn't change when we shifted to SUGAR and that belief won't change, no matter how big SUGAR becomes,' she says.

This view not only determined Vineeta's business proposition, it carried through to her marketing and the way her brand talked to its customers. For Vineeta, honesty with her core customer and a focus on her aspirations means the world. Very early on, she had decided that she would not build her new brand by discounting products but by using social media to educate young customers who were hesitant about buying make-up.

As a result, SUGAR Cosmetics has managed to make it to one of the top three colour cosmetics brands in India.[4]

So, when should you pivot? When is it time to call it quits on an idea that's struggling? A founder-entrepreneur talks to the consumer every day, trying to understand their patterns of using products or services. Most entrepreneurs swear by their gut feeling when it comes to judging if something is about to explode or if it's going to turn out to be a dud. 'You know exactly when to pivot when every additional sale forces you to work harder rather than things becoming easier by the day,' she says. 'Is it easier or harder to get every additional consumer? Are people lining up to get it or are you having to really shove it down their throats?'

An entrepreneur must have their ear to the ground when it comes to customer feedback. According to Vineeta, fantastic products and services have a powerfully positive word-of-mouth reach, and high referral velocity makes it progressively easier to acquire every additional customer. If that is not happening, it may be time to think about a pivot.

Another important thing to keep a tab on is how much in the way of losses you can absorb and calculate how much of a runway (that is, the number of months the start-up can keep operating before it runs out of money) you have, given your burn rate.

Vineeta adds that she had ₹30 lakh in her bank account – not enough to keep things going for even a year, in case she couldn't find financing, when she launched SUGAR. 'We had to solve problems and think about ways to fund it, pay salaries and, more importantly, determine whether there is a future in it or not,' she says.

LESSON 4

Building unshakeable confidence

Every Shark has one common quality. One magic power. 'As founders, we're the most optimistic people in the world because you need a certain amount of madness to build anything great. Otherwise you just give up on day one,' she explains. According to many entrepreneurs, this optimism can sometimes be borderline delusional. The thin line between ordinary optimism and that winning madness can be bridged by keeping a catchy millennial mantra in mind: 'Fake it till you make it'.

In his book, *The Magic of Thinking Big*, first published in 1959, author and motivational speaker, David J. Schwartz wrote: **'Act the part and you will become the part.'**[5] The idea behind the saying is that by acting as if you already have the confidence, skills and knowledge that you desire, you will eventually acquire them. Vineeta understands how important the 'fake it till you make it' attitude is in entrepreneurship.

'There are areas where it's very important to fake it until you make it. For example, in building confidence for us to be able to sell anything, whether we're selling it to an employee or to an investor or to a consumer. We have to reflect a very strong belief in a future which doesn't yet exist, and to be able to paint something which is vivid – you need to have really visualized it and believed in it,' she elaborates. 'You need a bit of overconfidence.'

But remember, there's self-confidence and then there are numbers like repeat rates, actual gross margin, EBITA (earnings before interest, taxes, depreciation and amortization), working capital cycles, etc. **'These are hard numbers and the best of entrepreneurs will not even**

exaggerate by a per cent because, at the end of the day, as an investor, you'll have trust issues. When you invest in a company, you're almost getting married to them. It's that kind of trust you need at that level,' she adds.

Entrepreneurs, she says, are like the greatest sales people of their businesses because it involves selling all the time. **'People become entrepreneurs to become their own boss. That's a misconception. You're actually not a boss. You're working for your investor, for your customer, for your employees. You're constantly selling and pitching.'**

So, while it's important to 'fake it till you make it', one needs to draw the line at hard numbers. 'As an entrepreneur, one should never misreport because the world is small and if one investor gets to know that there is a due diligence issue, it spreads like wildfire and then as an entrepreneur one becomes fundamentally uninvestable,' she adds.

> ' In life, we never regret the risks we take; we actually only regret the risks we did not take. I would rather take large risks than have large regrets. '

LESSON 5

The art of bouncing back

Kaushik recently shared a seven-year-old picture that brought back a plethora of memories of the tough days when the duo was still struggling to find funding. In that picture, Vineeta is lying on a bed with a pillow covering her face because she had been crying for an hour or so.

A large, well-reputed venture capital fund was supposed to invest in the company, but at the last moment the deal didn't go through because they weren't sure about the market size and SUGAR's potential to scale. At that point of time, there were very few months of runway left. Without that funding, there was every chance that the business could shut down.

'I have had a hundred other rejections from VCs but a lot was at stake here. When it didn't come through, I knew I had to cry it out. There's so much emotion within me that needs to come out. It's a part of my recovery process,' she says.

She cried for over two hours that day. The next day, to everyone's surprise, she was back in hurricane mode, asking questions like: How much money is left? Should we relook our marketing strategy? How should we rebuild this?

'Had I not cried that day, it would have stressed me out, and then I would have probably lost sleep over it. And there would have been all other kinds of physical reactions. I feel it's a very powerful coping mechanism.'

Start-up founders may feel the pressure to appear strong and capable, which often makes them reluctant to admit to any weaknesses or vulnerabilities, or discuss their mental health openly. Another reason for this is the 'start-up culture', which makes a cult out of the importance of hard work and perseverance. For some founders, this can create a mindset where admitting to fragility or mental health issues is seen as a sign of weakness or failure.

As a result, **many start-up founders stay mum about mental health issues for fear of being judged, or being seen as less competent**. Poor mental health can not only affect a person's ability to think clearly, make decisions and solve problems – all of which are crucial skills for a start-up founder – but it can also lead to communication issues, misunderstandings and conflicts, which may end up hurting the start-up.

As the ecosystem evolves, mentally healthy workplaces are being given the due attention they deserve, and founders like Vineeta have been at the forefront of this change. She says that for a lot of women who work at SUGAR, it often happens that whenever they are in a situation where someone is being unfair or argumentative, more often than not, a generalized reaction is to start shaking, instead of being aggressive and raising their voices, like most men would. Vineeta has also spoken out about the need for normalizing crying at workplaces.

'I cry a lot at work and every single time that happens, I realize that my colleagues, at least the men, look at it as a form of weakness, a breakdown. Whereas if somebody just raised their voice or argued or became aggressive, it would have been seen as a symbol of strength,' she observes.

It's a misconception, she says, that she can't take the pressure. In fact, she avers, 'I've seen that because women are able to have this outlet where they are able to cry it out, they are very strong when they are done with it. I found that there is a big power in crying out a failure or a setback. It should be encouraged at work, and managers should understand that it's a form of communication and they should take it like that, rather than as a breakdown.'

Vineeta has normalized crying as a mechanism to deal with stressful situations. **'I cry when I feel like crying, when I'm having an argument I cannot handle, when a situation gets too stressful. And I'm the strongest person I know,'** she says. 'I don't think crying takes away from your strength, and women may cry at the drop of a hat; it's important that the people we work with get that.'

Vineeta's fundas

According to Vineeta, figuring out the founder-market fit is a starting point. Every entrepreneur needs to gauge what they're good at, and check if the market requires those skills.

'My first business, which I ended up starting because my lingerie brand didn't get funding, was a B2B [business to business] company. I am terrible at B2B sales and services, and I did not have a founder-market fit because I'm not passionate about it. Every day it used to feel like a drag, whereas I love what I'm building now,' she says.

Secondly, she adds, one needs to figure out the right person to run the business because if there's somebody else better than you, then you should be doing something else.

'Keep tweaking,' Vineeta says, until such time as you figure out the product-market fit. 'You can change 100 million times after getting feedback to ensure that you have created the right product and then solve for cash flow, which means that if it's going to lose some money in the beginning, raise some capital, or build profitability,' she says.

You must keep cash flow in mind while running the business. Businesses are not just profit-driven; cash flow is required to sustain any company. The next important thing after figuring out the cash flow is building a great team. 'If you don't build a great team, then all the other things will not matter. You have to hire people smarter than you and empower them. Get them excited about the business. I think these are the steps by which you reduce your chances of failing,' she adds. 'But you can still fail. It's a big lie when a founder says they did it on their own. I think all of us got lucky.'

For SUGAR, there was a huge excitement around brands coming out of India, and D2C, or direct to consumer, was just opening up. 'Anybody who says luck didn't have a role to play hasn't really failed enough number of times.'

VINEETA'S GUIDE TO STARTING A START-UP

- If you want your start-up to work, play the long game. Aim for the 'did not quit' medal.
- Be prepared to lose everything.
- If things aren't working – pivot, don't quit.
- Don't be afraid to be emotional.
- Fake your confidence ...
- ... But don't fake your numbers.

2

Aman Gupta and His Three BFs: Be Fast, Fearless and Frugal

'When we started our business, frugality wasn't a choice; it was our only option. And now it has become a habit.'

Picture a fourth standard English school exam with the question 'Use "boat" in a sentence'. Most students would write an answer along the lines of 'a vehicle for travelling on water'. But conventions are constantly changing, right? And young student Anvay, whose answer sheet went viral, is testament to the fact that shows like *Shark Tank* have managed to touch the minds of young, impressionable Indians like nothing else. As an answer to that question, Anvay wrote 'boat is a brand of headphones by Aman Gupta'. Aman was quick to share the post on his Instagram saying, 'A for Apple B for boAt. Petition to make this change in all textbooks.'[1]

Well, not sure about the change in the textbooks, but the change in mindset when it comes to entrepreneurship has already begun, all thanks to self-made entrepreneurs like Aman.

One of Aman's major contributions to the entrepreneurship ecosystem is his unabashedly frugal mindset. Return on investment (ROI), he says, is always at the back of his mind, and sometimes even when there's no financial investment involved! Yet, despite its importance, frugality as a concept is hardly talked about in entrepreneurship circles, which seem to focus more on boardroom gossip and textbook concepts like ideation, market research and expansion.

Being frugal does not mean being cheap or 'jugadu'. It is about being resourceful and finding creative ways to meet one's needs. Take one of Aman's role models, Jeff Bezos. He may have a net worth of over $100 billion, but he swears by frugality. He believes constrained resources drive innovation, since the best way to get out of a tight box is to invent your way out. And if you can embrace it, you will be on the path to sustainability and profitability – the only path to be.

WHO IS AMAN GUPTA?

Shark Aman Gupta is a CA by training. The 40-year-old worked with CitiBank and KPMG before going to the Kellogg School of Management to acquire an MBA. He also worked with JBL and other consumer electronics brands.

In 2014, he and his co-founder Sameer Mehta bootstrapped and launched boAt by investing ₹30 lakh each from their own pockets. It was like a match made in heaven. Aman brought his aggressiveness while Sameer came with his structured approach. boAt offers a range of audio earwear, True Wireless

Stereo (TWS) tech, smartwatches and travel chargers and other personal electronics products. With boAt Labs – the in-house R&D team – boAt now designs, engineers and, with the support of global players, has started manufacturing products in India.

The new start-up boAt hit ₹100 crore in revenues within a couple of years of launch. The Qualcomm-backed company had a stock buyback during 2020–21 of about ₹140 crore, with Aman and Sameer receiving ₹56.8 crore each. It is now India's No. 1 and the world's No. 2 wearable gadgets company as per the International Data Corporation (IDC) in Q3CY2022.[2] In FY22, it logged a revenue of ₹2,873 crore with ₹68.7 crore in profits.[3] boAt has also raised $165 million to date from prolific investors, including Warburg Pincus, Malabar Investments and Fireside Ventures.[4]

LESSON I

Make ROI your mantra

Let's return to frugality and try to understand why it has worked for boAt and how Aman's frugal and agile management style has even made boAt the subject of a case study at the Harvard Business School.

Frugality, Aman feels, is at the core of the company's business model. He can cite so many examples of when this attitude has worked for him. Take his first office, for example. They worked out of a co-working space in SOCIAL at Delhi's Hauz Khas. 'We used to pay ₹5,000 a month for five seats. We would get food and drink coupons. For ₹25,000 a month, we could get loads of work clubbed with loads of entertainment,' he says.

Even today, when he can afford an office in the more plush parts of Gurugram, he preferred to go through tedious negotiation sessions with the builders of Udyog Vihar, which is a cheaper locality, 12 minutes away from the premium business district. 'If there's frugality in everything you do, you'll be able to create value for stakeholders.'

In another instance, when he had to book a luxury car rental – which costs upwards of ₹30,000 – for one of his brand ambassadors, he quickly took to Facebook to ask if any of his friends can lend him an appropriate vehicle and he ended up saving on that expense. 'People look at marketing and say 50% of marketing is wasted; I look at it and try to ensure that 90% should not be wasted,' he says.

Whenever he has to spend money in the business he asks a simple question – is it a return on investment? Would it make a difference if the office worked out of a cheaper area in Gurugram? What are the marketing decisions that are truly effective?

But surely wondering too much about profitability

hampers growth in the early days of a company? There is no one-size-fits-all answer to this. The ideal balance will depend on the specific circumstances of the start-up and the goals of the founder. Some start-ups may prioritize growth at the expense of profitability in the early stages, while others may prioritize profitability from the outset.

For the boAt founders, focusing on one or the other was never an option. 'I didn't have an option but to focus on both growth and profitability. Whatever business we did, we had to sell profitably. We didn't have funding. If we weren't profitable, we had to put in our own money. Frugality was our only option. We had to learn to run our company on less,' he says.

Ultimately, the key is to find a balance between the two that allows the start-up to achieve both short-term and long-term success. Growth is important because it helps a start-up to establish a strong market presence and reach a wider customer base. This can be achieved through various methods, such as marketing and sales efforts, product development, partnerships, etc. At the same time, profitability is also important because it ensures that the start-up is financially sustainable and able to generate sufficient revenue to cover its expenses and invest in future growth.

Aman's company has been profitable since inception and boAt continues its dominance in the wearables and wireless audio accessories segment in India. The company registered over 2X growth in its scale for two consecutive fiscal years: FY21 and FY22.[5] The company registered a revenue of ₹2,873 crore in FY22 and posted ₹68.7 crore in profits.[6]

In the early years, when funds were short, Aman would ask his wife to visit stores in various parts of Delhi and ask for boAt earphones. By creating this artificial demand, he leveraged the fear of missing out (FOMO) to his advantage. Shopkeepers were convinced that if they didn't stock his products, they would miss the boat (pun intended).

LESSON 2

Just like love, find yourself the right co-founder

Some founders go it alone. But many of you will need support – one or a few partners in crime. The Bansals of Flipkart, Vineeta Singh and her husband Kaushik. The examples are endless. Running a start-up is a stressful business and you will need a partner in crime for all the hard times.

But your co-founder will also play another big role. For Aman, the complementary mindset of his co-founder has been crucial. 'Had Sameer been the only person running boAt's operations, the company would never have started; had I been the only person, it would have been too aggressive and would have probably been shut by now. **Sameer and I balance each other,'** Aman says.

'It's like yin and yang. People like me need a co-founder. I'm too aggressive, and Sameer was needed to make it a success. My strengths are building relationships and sales. Sameer does the things I hate doing,' he says laughingly.

Typically, co-founders know each other well. When they decide to venture into a new business, they're either siblings, a couple or very good friends, but Sameer and Aman hardly knew each other when they decided to work to start boAt. They met through a common connection and soon realized that both of them were interested in building a brand of their own. 'He knew distribution and backend very well, and I knew frontend very well. It was more like bringing our complementary skills together, but it was a very risky bet,' Aman said in the podcast *The Barber Shop*.

Aman's father has had a history with a partnership gone wrong. This is another point common to both Aman and Sameer. Sameer, too, had an incident where he had a bad run with a partner. 'It is more like an arranged marriage, that too a long-distance one because I'm in Delhi and Sameer operates out of Mumbai,' Aman says.

Looking back, Aman feels that the decision to work together could have gone either way.

Sameer heads finance, products, and logistics and operations, while Aman heads sales and marketing. 'He reports to me for his line functions, but I report to him for my functions. Sometimes there are disagreements but it's a circular relationship between us. I hate what he's doing; he hates what I'm doing. That's why we work so well together,' Aman says. In fact, Sony first approached Sameer to be a judge on *Shark Tank India*, but he didn't like the limelight, so he recommended Aman instead. That's the kind of partnership that would make even seasoned couples envious, ain't it?

> ' I'm one of the best people in terms of understanding the consumer very well. I'm a consumer-centric guy; I look at a common man. I talk to a lot of people. I am inspired by the youth. I observe them, understand their influences and give them the product they need. '

LESSON 3

Find a Product Market Fit (PMF)

boAt is ranked No. 2 in the overall wearables market as per leading market research and advisory firm IDC's Worldwide

Quarterly Wearable Device Tracker Q3CY2022.[7] At the core of this success was the positioning. Consider India's wireless earphone industry when boAt entered the game:

Ultra-premium category	₹15,000 and above	Bose, Apple
Premium category	₹10,000–₹15,000	JBL
Sub-premium category	₹5,000–₹10,000	Sennheiser
Economy/Affordable	₹1,000–₹5,000	boAt

When boAt entered, the affordable category only had niche or relatively unknown brands. There were more than 200 brands in that category, including a plethora of Chinese, Japanese, German and Indian players. Through influencer marketing and by getting faces like Hardik Pandya, Kartik Aaryan, Neha Kakkar, etc., to endorse its products, boAt was able to stand out in that category.

'There was no fun when I was working at JBL because the markets were changing, and the company was not as receptive to the changing market. That's where I felt there's a good opportunity to build a brand. Digital was starting up, it was less capital intensive, distribution was very easy, digital branding was becoming better,' he says.

'Looking at all these possibilities, it was a good time. There's a right age for understanding the right consumer.

We priced the product right. India ko bass pasand hai (India likes bass), so we designed a bass-heavy headphone. We did all the right things. We did not have super abnormal margins, kept the price right. And boom!'

LESSON 4

Learn from your failures

Aman swears by the things he learnt from failed ventures. One of them was not building a lean start-up from the get-go. 'It was a mistake to have too many structures,' he says. '**People can do much more when you don't compartmentalize them.** The second learning was to do customer relationship management better. B2B needs to have very good customer management; we have to manage relationships with Amazon, Flipkart, Nykaa, Croma, Reliance, etc. It's all about people management.'

Having worked at legacy companies before advancing to the forefront of India's start-up revolution, Aman has many learnings as takeaways. '**Start-ups have to learn from legacy companies. How to make money, how to run big companies, how to think in a structured manner. Legacy companies need to learn from start-ups how to be nimble,'** he says.

Embracing failures, he explains, made all the difference. 'I don't think you need two–three successes; you need one success. **I've had five failures, but one success has made me who I am,'** he says.

> 'I'm a common man, a middle-class guy, and I feel that an entrepreneur should be grounded first and foremost. Hustle is my way of life. I don't ask everyone to hustle but I relate to people who hustle. Nowadays, entrepreneurs get a spotlight in the media and there's a God syndrome that kicks in. That's very bad for the company and the entire ecosystem. Be ready for ups, be ready for downs. But be yourself.'

LESSON 5

Go on, and have a never-say-die attitude

Early on in his life, Aman got a lesson from his father – himself an entrepreneur – on keeping his ego aside while making sales calls. This persistence and never-say-die attitude is what got Aman his first funding, led by Kanwaljit Singh of Fireside Ventures, after facing multiple rejections by investors, banks and even potential employees who refused to join the company with an 'uncertain' future.

boAt raised ₹6 crore in funding from Fireside Ventures in its first round. 'I kept pursuing Kanwal and shamelessly sending him reminders on LinkedIn. One fine day, he agreed to meet me. We closed the deal over the breakfast table. I've been very persuasive in what I want. Just like my personal life. My wife was not agreeing to marry me but I eventually wore her down,' he jokes.

As everyone around him kept getting funded, Aman kept getting rejections until Fireside happened. 'The key is to keep your expectations low during such times. I never dreamt of running a company and being where I am. I'm living a dream that I never saw; maybe I'm living someone else's dream. I never dreamt that boAt would be the No.2 wearables brand in the world after Apple – **I just set out to stay happy, providing customers with the right products**,' he says.

There is, however, a fine line between overconfidence and what Aman got famous for saying in Season 1 of *Shark Tank*: 'Hum bhi bana lengay' (we will also make it), in response to a fellow Shark's claim of making a big-buck business. 'Yes, there's a thin line. If you don't have confidence, then never do anything. People don't know what lies inside them, they don't know what they're good at. Start-ups fail because sometimes entrepreneurs become delusional, and they don't keep up with change. The engine of innovation needs to keep running,' he says.

'I'm very paranoid about my competition. If I can come and disrupt, somebody else can come and disrupt me too. **The Davids can be Goliaths and the Goliaths can be Davids. The only thing that helps one sail through is customer obsession,**' Aman observes.

Shark Tank: A dream come true

But entrepreneurship, he adds, is not everyone's cup of tea. 'You should #DoWhatFloatsYourboAt – a philosophy we swear by. My wife started a business but ended it in six months because she cannot take the stress of 24-hour work days,' he notes.

Shows like *Shark Tank* have helped Aman in his entrepreneurial journey. It's a full-circle moment for him and a way of giving back to the community by becoming a Shark on *Shark Tank India*. '*Shark Tank* has helped people like me. Now its Indian version is helping millions of others. People are learning and getting the right type of education. These lessons are very important to build India's awareness towards the start-up ecosystem,' he says.

He adds that pre-*Shark Tank India*, entrepreneurship was not celebrated as much as it is today. Post the show, it's not only that his brand has benefited, he has also enjoyed the personal fame that has come with it.

'**Never say no to free marketing,**' says the man who keeps frugality as his mantra. 'The upside of the show is that people are buying more of my products because they loved me on the show. **I love the fame and attention and sales that the brand has got with it.** In India, business is not as widely discussed as a subject, but the show made sure it's not taboo anymore. The downside, however, is that people think we write cheques in 10 minutes. I find elevator pitches everywhere I go. I had people approaching me in washrooms,' he jokes.

How Aman invests

'I bet on the person,' Aman has said in almost every pitch across two seasons. Aman – who turned into an investor for the first time on *Shark Tank India* – says that he didn't know much about investing before the show and wasn't a seasoned investor like Anupam or the other Sharks. 'I didn't know investment, but I know people. I'm a people person. I invest in the person who's in front of me who's trying to sincerely build a business.'

Even on the sets of *Shark Tank India*, Aman can be seen being pally with almost everybody on the set, and he genuinely enjoys the company of different kinds of people. This is probably why he was personally in touch with his first few consumers when he launched the brand to understand the challenges they were facing. He likes to invest in people with a similar mindset, saying, **'If I get a glimpse of me in the founder, I will invest in that person.'** As a result, on the show, he has never fought for the price or that extra stake, focusing instead on whether the founder found value in getting him onboard and vice versa.

Aman says that the companies that he invested in because of FOMO, because another Shark had invested in them, have done badly. On the other hand, the companies that he invested in because he believed in the business and the founder have done very well. 'I invested in those companies because I saw myself in them and it's going very well for me.'

Sometimes he has got it wrong too. '*Shark Tank* gives huge exposure to companies that either get investment, free advice, or publicity when they come on it. Companies become national brands overnight after appearing on the show. As an investor, sometimes you regret not investing in good companies, like I didn't invest in JhaJi pickles and they've done very well.'

Investing isn't a science. It's a gut thing, even a situational thing. Aman says that there are so many things that are going on in the mind of a Shark at any given time. 'Sometimes you've done six deals in the morning and by night your appetite is over. Sometimes you hear so much negativity from other Sharks, you feel you don't want to make a mistake by investing, you feel you might take the wrong step. There are a thousand thoughts that cross your mind, but you have to make a decision right there and then.'

Naturally, he and the other Sharks haven't always got it right. If you are looking for investment, remember that who chooses to back you could be a gut thing, but also about where the investor is at the moment. There are all kinds of factors at play which you may not have any control over. You simply must give it your best shot and keep your fingers crossed.

AMAN'S GUIDE TO STARTING A START-UP

- ROI – focus on unit economics and financial management
- Hustle – be industrious, work smart and build relationships
- Build and invest in a good team
- Grahak bhagwan hai (Customer is God) – aim for delivering the best customer experience
- As a start-up founder, it's important to make ethics a cornerstone of your business.
- Starting a successful business can be an incredible ego boost, but the key is to stay humble throughout the journey.

3

Why Peyush Bansal Thinks Empathy Is His Secret Weapon

'Empathy is the difference between building a business and building an impactful organization.'

What's common to a rental in a one-bedroom apartment in New York City, a Hermes Birkin handbag and a bottle of Clive Christian perfume? Well, they all cost roughly ₹10 lakh each.

That same amount can also change the lives of thousands of small farmers by giving them an innovative product that will help them manage the critical problems of pest control. And that is precisely how 'Jugaadu Kamlesh', as Kamlesh Nanasaheb Ghumare of Malegaon in Maharashtra is known, is using it.

Kamlesh's appearance on *Shark Tank India* Season 1 became the most watched pitch of the season. It was probably the first and only time (so far) audiences got teary-eyed watching an investment deal.

Kamlesh's presentation showed how, without too many resources, he had designed and built a pesticide cart. This was to help farmers like his father. It saved them the trouble of carrying a 17-litre tank strapped to their backs as they walked through the fields spraying pesticide. It greatly reduced the danger of inhaling toxic pesticides.

'Jugaad' can perhaps be translated to 'a hack' or 'a workaround'. It is often used in the context of entrepreneurship and business, where it refers to the ability to improvise and find creative solutions to challenges in resource-constrained environments.

'Jugaad innovation' is characterized by resourcefulness, flexibility and the ability to adapt to constraints. It involves finding creative solutions by using whatever resources are available, rather than by following traditional textbook methods. Kamlesh's cart is a classic example of jugaad – a cheap, effective way to ease farming practices. No wonder he had chosen to call himself 'Jugaadu Kamlesh' on the show.

But Lenskart's Peyush Bansal was impressed by another quality in Kamlesh – what he called his empathy. He invested ₹10 lakh for 40% equity, also throwing in a flexible, no-interest loan of ₹20 lakh in Kamlesh's company, K.G. Agrotech. He was the only Shark to invest in the business. As he says, **'Empathy is a key pillar. You need empathy towards your shareholders, customers, investors; lack of empathy is a big-scale deterrent as well.'**

When you think of the qualities you will need to achieve success in your business, you'll think of resilience, hard work, adaptability, speed. You probably won't think of the word empathy. Empathy means imagining yourself in someone else's shoes. Thinking to yourself, what if I were them. It's this philosophy that colours Peyush's approach to his business and one that he believes has led to his success.

WHO IS PEYUSH BANSAL?

The 38-year-old founder of Lenskart studied Electrical Engineering at Canada's McGill University and worked for Microsoft for about a year before launching 'searchmycampus.com' with an initial investment of ₹25 lakh. It aggregated links to many services used by college students. But in December 2008, he closed searchmycampus.com and headed to IIM Bangalore.

In November 2010, Peyush Bansal and his co-founders Amit Chaudhary, Sumeet Kapahi and Neha Bansal launched Lenskart, which specializes in eyewear and offers its entire range online and offline.

So far, Lenskart has raised funding through multiple investors, including TPG, Chiratae Ventures, the Softbank Vision Fund, KKR, Temasek and more up to a Series I round.[1]

LESSON I

Why having empathy is a key ingredient for success

For Peyush, it's almost impossible to build a business without empathy. 'There's a difference between building a business and building an impactful organization. Empathy is a key pillar in the process of solving a core problem, taking a long-term view and having laser-sharp focus on the goal. You need empathy towards your shareholders, customers, investors; **lack of empathy is a big-scale deterrent as well.**'

Empathy and integrity also affect his investing decisions. 'Investing is fundamentally based on trust. There can only be a line of communication between you (the investor) and the entrepreneur, and it's the entrepreneur who talks to the company. The value systems, honesty, integrity and transparency of the entrepreneurs are at the core of it all,' he says. Honesty about yourself as an entrepreneur, he believes, is another core value foundational to building a business.

There are people who think of investor money as third-party money. **'You've got to treat investor money more carefully than your own money because there's a moral obligation. Some entrepreneurs understand this.** Some entrepreneurs think it's their opportunity cost, and in case the business doesn't work, they always have an option to take up a job. They don't feel the pain of investor money.'

Peyush took to LinkedIn to explain why he invested in Kamlesh. He wrote:

'This is why I think he is a rockstar entrepreneur:

1. Big vision and purpose: He said he wants to *solve all* problems that farmers face. He was speaking about

electric, seed dropping, what all not . . . *badi soch!* [big thinking!]

2. Real problem: The problem he is trying to solve is real . . . a 17-litre tank on the farmer's back + pesticides going into eyes and nose.
3. Passionate: The way he spoke, I could see passion flowing from every inch of his body . . . I had goosebumps!
4. Perseverance: He has been at it for seven years and still has not given up. He even found a way to come to the Tank.
5. Agility and desire to learn: He is willing to fail and learn and fail again. He had to change the design multiple times to get to this final design, and he was sure if someone supports [him], he can make it even better.
6. Positivity: **One cannot change the world with a negative view.** This is Kamlesh's biggest strength in my view. When I asked him how he was feeling after not getting a deal, his answer was "I am feeling very good." He seriously had me there . . .
7. Confidence and respect: The way he walked into the Tank and handed over his card with confidence, the use of "JUGAADU" in his name and way he thanked everyone and complimented Namita in the end (he

even thanked the Sharks who did not give him a deal . . . very rare), shows how respectful he is.

8. Customer empathy: He was really feeling the pain of the farmers, I could see [it] in his eyes. He kept saying "farmers work 24 hours". He feels the pain from his heart. When asked "why not use a trolley", he clearly knew the reasons why and this is because he understands the ground reality.
9. Team player: He said he can employ youth in the village and appreciated Naru [a boy from the village who helped him with the project and accompanied him to *Shark Tank*] . . . this is a very rare, yet super important quality, as companies are not built by ideas but by people and recognizing their effort!
10. Last and most important for me – values and humility: Kamlesh has given Naru a stake in the company, and he said to me, "I can't leave Naru out and he will be there with me always." He was telling me whatever I do, Naru has to be there; else he is out. Only someone who is humble can say that, and with so much clarity.'

'The empathy is not so much for him as for the fact that others have the privilege of having some of, what we call, luck available. It takes empathy to give someone that opportunity, an equal fair chance. I can't make him

a better entrepreneur; he's already one. It's about giving him a level playing field,' Peyush remarks.

LESSON 2

Your start-up journey is unique to you

How do I get started on my start-up journey? Should I quit my current job and focus on building the business? Or just do it on the side until my finances are more secure?

When young entrepreneurs ask Peyush about the 'right time' to quit a job to start a business, he has no glib answers. 'Deciding when to quit your current job to start your own company is a personal and complex decision that requires careful consideration. There is no one-size-fits-all answer, as it will depend on one's individual circumstances and goals,' he says.

Starting a company can be a risky and uncertain venture, so it's important to ensure that you have the financial resources to support yourself and your family during the early stages of your business. This may involve saving up money, having a solid business plan and seeking out investment or funding opportunities.

A significant time and energy commitment is another prerequisite, so it's important to be sure you are ready and willing to take on this challenge. Consider whether you have the passion and drive to pursue your business idea and handle the ups and downs of entrepreneurship. Remember, empathy is the key word here. Have empathy for yourself, your personality and circumstances.

'There's no fixed rule,' Peyush says. 'There are entrepreneurs who quit employment before starting their venture, and then there are those who quit at the early stage of the idea and some after it has gotten to a certain stage. I think, ideally, once you've figured out a space and a problem and you have a fair idea of what you want to do, it's not too bad to quit employment because then you're 100% focused,' he observes.

'When I quit, I was gambling with a few ideas. **The downside of doing it on the side is that if your job is very demanding, it becomes a big deterrent and you always have a fallback option so that paranoia and hunger doesn't come in.** I almost quit before I started, but I had some idea of what I wanted to do.'

This also applies to the question about when to fundraise. With *Shark Tank India*'s success, Peyush feels that people who were sitting on the edge have jumped into the ecosystem and now want to make their businesses bigger than they would have earlier aspired to.

So, when should you look for investment? He feels that there's no right time or wrong time. You might be happy to bootstrap your start-up till you see some proof of success. Others might want to raise at the get-go, while there are many successful businesses that choose to fundraise only when they are mature. It goes back to what the entrepreneur wants to build in the long term and whether a given investment will help them achieve that. 'If 10 years down the line, the business matters and you've made the desired impact, then you take it. If an investment is coming at a time when it will increase the probability of success, and that's what matters to the entrepreneur, then to each his own,' he says.

LESSON 3

Align your investors well

1. Some investors may be more focused on short-term returns and may push for decisions that prioritize immediate profits over long-term growth. Here, it is important to align.
2. Potential conflict: If you have multiple investors with different priorities and goals, it can lead to conflicts and difficulties in decision-making.

Before you take investor money, you should align them with your vision and ways of growing. **'If you make something of true value and meaning, then money will follow. But if you follow money, nothing happens. You have to chase value creation in what you're doing,'** Peyush says.

Everything, he says, depends on the entrepreneur. '**This person has to drive the show.** An investor is investing for the entrepreneur. Without a great entrepreneur, there's no execution. A lot of times you overevaluate ideas but you can pivot if nothing's working,' he says.

'You must evaluate whether it's a business-driven objective, versus a mission-driven objective,' he says. 'You can't be confused as an entrepreneur and leave it open-ended for others.'

It's not just important to have money, it's also important to align the agenda and ask the investor what their expectations are,' he says.

Even today, he grapples with the question of raising money. In 2019, Lenskart raised $275 million from the Softbank Vision Fund. Some of the existing investors were against the decision but Peyush and his co-founders wanted it to happen. 'We felt what we were doing was phenomenal but this could put us in a different orbit in terms of capability and would allow us to think long-term. **Put the company first, investors second, yourself third, and things will often fall in place.**'

Even here, empathy helps. Now, being a Shark and an investor himself, he tries to better understand the other side of the story. '**I think most investors don't want to interfere but entrepreneurs sometimes don't leave them with a choice. They're confused, and don't want to take**

the ownership of the good and bad calls. We can stop blaming investors for some time! They're the ones whose money is at stake.'

WHAT YOU NEED TO KNOW ABOUT YOUR INVESTOR

According to Inc42, in 2021 'Seed funding worth $1.1 billion was initiated in India with an average deal size of $2.3 million.'[2] The world of investments is changing like never before. People who've historically never even invested in public markets are investing in private markets because they believe in the Indian entrepreneurship dream.

As you move in your start-up journey you need to pay attention to the investor and spend some time researching. What sort of investor is investing in which type of business? Whom should I be pitching to in order to succeed? What are their views and approaches?

Research the investor's portfolio and focus areas, and look at the types of companies and industries they have previously invested in. Make sure you understand what factors are important to them and how the company fits with those criteria. It is also important to clearly and concisely communicate the value of the company to potential investors. The entrepreneur should clearly be able to articulate their business model, target market and growth potential, etc.

LESSON 4

Pivoting is not failure

Like all our Sharks, Lenskart wasn't Peyush's first business. From IT to college logistics to eyewear – he's made a lot of shifts!

His college logistics business, searchmycampus, already had 1,500 colleges registered with the portal, but Peyush soon realized that from an impact perspective, that's as far as it could go. 'The problem I was trying to solve with the portal wasn't such a big problem that you could continue to work on it and scale up for that long. When I realized that, it was the trigger point for me to try something new.'

He says that one has to be open to failure but also be honest. Like Vineeta, Peyush too believes pivoting isn't quitting. **'You should know when to pivot. Giving up is the wrong word – pivoting is not failure.'**

Typically, according to Peyush, it should take three to six months for an entrepreneur to understand if it's the right problem or the right solution. 'Scalability and the size of the market – one will get to know in about a year.'

As confirmed by Ross Geller in the American sitcom, *F.R.I.E.N.D.S.*, a pivot can be a risky move. It involves making significant changes to the direction of the business, and while many ailing businesses revive because of a timely pivot, many others shut down because of a pivot gone wrong.

Peyush says, a pivot is just the stepping stone, a comma in the whole process. It's all about taking a step back and being open to the view that maybe one was not so right about either the problem or the solution and its execution.

Thankfully, in the case of Lenskart, the impact of a pivot was positive. Soon after Lenskart launched in November 2010, the company diversified into different categories like bags, jewellery and watches. 'We thought glasses weren't that much of a problem back then.' In the next four years, Peyush realized the value they were creating in eyewear was 10x that of the other lines.

'We listened to the customers and shut down all other businesses. **The wow factor and the word of mouth in eyewear category was much higher, which meant we had found a problem area and people got the solution, and they were talking about it. That really told us that we're onto something big. I think the key here is to observe carefully, and be honest and transparent,**' he explains.

'It's important to observe without (directly) asking the consumers. You have to pretty much put your ego aside and not be attached to your idea. It gets quite lonely. Even when we were shutting down these businesses, it was a big decision and could have gone either way. **While success belongs to everybody, failure is usually the entrepreneur's.**'

Such moments can be hard for a founder. 'Not all these decisions can be democratic decisions, especially starting and shutting down businesses. Why it becomes lonely is when you take those decisions, the entrepreneur has to take accountability and own it fully.' He remarks that even his team were tempted during these periods to quit and take up safe jobs.

'Knowing what I know now, I would not start Jewelskart, Bagskart and Watchkart. But some learnings have come along the way and maybe we got a team because of these categories, which then started working for Lenskart,' he says.

But Peyush also warns that 'there's a difference between being persistent and being blind'. Being persistent means continuing to achieve a goal or desired outcome, despite setbacks or obstacles. It involves being determined and resilient in the face of challenges and not giving up easily. On the other hand, being delusional means holding on to a belief or idea despite clear evidence to the contrary.

'If your gut is telling you that your solution is being talked about by people but sales are still low, then maybe you look at the sales methodology, or the person you've empowered to carry that particular function. **Then you need to be persistent about it, but if there's a problem in the problem itself, then it's wise to give up. It's a very fine**

balance,' he explains. **'Sometimes, success is on the other side of the line but you never know that.'**

Even today, Peyush struggles with finding the right answers. 'There are so many times we're starting new businesses, starting new geographies and shutting them. "What if" is a bad space to be in,' he says.

LESSON 5

Hire for potential not experience

Soon after Season 1 got over, Yarn Bazaar founder Pratik Gadia, reached out to his investor Peyush for advice on hiring a co-founder. Peyush feels 99% of entrepreneurs come to him for advice on who and how to hire.

'My only intervention with Pratik was that he shouldn't go for somebody who has been there and done that or just because that person's resume looks good, but rather go for somebody who he thinks he can work with,' he states.

'Hire for your cultural fitment versus the best resume. **If you want to open 1,000 stores, you don't need someone who has opened 1,000 stores, you need somebody with a potential to open 1,000 stores.** Experience is not a big quality to have if you're looking for someone to hire for a start-up.'

LESSON 6

Find a mentor

Peyush says *Shark Tank India* has been a great learning experience for him, not just as an investor but also as a mentor, for he wasn't the latter earlier. Mentors, he feels, can play a valuable role in the success of a start-up and its founders.

Starting and growing a company can be a demanding and stressful process. A mentor can help you to stay motivated and focused on your goals while offering a fresh perspective and providing objective feedback.

Mentors typically have experience and expertise in a particular field or industry and can provide valuable guidance and advice based on their own experiences, helping founders navigate the challenges of starting and growing a business. They can also help introduce founders to potential partners, investors, customers and other key players in their industry. These connections can be invaluable in helping a start-up succeed.

For Peyush, the entrepreneur and entertainment magnate Ronnie Screwvala has been a key player in his start-up journey. '**There shouldn't be more than one or two mentors, otherwise you get conflicting viewpoints.** I have often gone back and shared problems about scale, people, teams, culture and mistakes with Ronnie. And I had the luxury of having him through the various stages of growth.'

Well, life has come full circle. Peyush had Ronnie, now budding entrepreneurs like Jugaadu Kamlesh have Peyush as a mentor as they embark on their own journeys.

LESSON 7

Great businesses take time to grow

Lenskart began with an aim to become the Maruti of Indian eyewear. 'We want 50% of India to wear our glasses.' According to Peyush, obsessing over the consumer versus obsessing about the competition paid off. 'We were really not bothered back then about what the competition was doing. We are a lot more bothered now.'

He also cautions that the desire to grow the company quarter-on-quarter is a big trap that comes in the way of fulfilling long-term goals. 'If you are free from the agenda that you've got to raise the next round because it's considered to be good, then you can focus on consumer needs. **Great businesses are not built overnight. That kind of approach is what allows it to become monopolistic in terms of market share and stay ahead of the curve,'** he says. 'At our stage also, many of the core problems are still unsolved. I would have just wanted to do that instead of getting into the quarterly, weekly and monthly performance ecosystem.'

It took Lenskart almost a decade to turn profitable in FY20. Peyush feels he spent the company's money on the right things. 'If you believe that your service is good and you're willing to be selling at a loss because you feel somebody could pay in the future, then that could work. In our business, the margin is probably the highest. Where we were burning money was largely investment in tech, infrastructure, factory, automation, building a brand, etc. One should be clear what you're spending on versus trying to sell at a loss or an inorganic way to get revenue,' he says.

There are many kinds of founders and many kinds of businesses. Peyush Bansal's dream is to create a lasting and genuinely impactful business that will affect all of India. But with such a long game in mind, you have to be patient and resilient, ready to weather every storm. Your investors have to support and understand you; you will need to find the right team who have the same vision and you must understand and know yourself. Now that's called empathy.

PEYUSH'S GUIDE TO STARTING A START-UP

- Build empathy in your team, for your investors and, above all, for your customers. Always put yourself in their shoes.
- There are no fixed rules about when and how to start-up or fundraise.
- In a start-up, hire for promise not experience.
- Find a mentor – but not too many of them.
- Recognize that being a founder is lonely – the hardest decisions are yours alone to make.

4

Namita Thapar's Success Mantra

'Being organized and being optimistic are the two things that help me wear multiple hats and balance work and life.'

Namita Thapar's punctuality is legendary. She's always the first person to show up at the Andheri West studios for a *Shark Tank* shoot. She's always the first guest to arrive at the wrap party post-shoot, and on one unforgettable occasion, she arrived at the party before the host did! This clockwork precision helps her run a ₹2,000-crore business, the Thapar Entrepreneurs Academy and a show called *Uncondition Yourself*, in addition to being a full-time mother!

How does she do it? By being organized and optimistic. These two qualities have helped her navigate her entire professional and personal life. 'Not just entrepreneurs, every person needs to have these,' she says. 'Being organized and being optimistic are the two things that help me wear multiple hats and balance work and life. Otherwise, it's not possible to stay calm amidst the madness of everyday life.'

WHO IS NAMITA THAPAR?

The 45-year-old CA from Pune is the Executive Director of Emcure Pharma, a large drug manufacturer set up by her father. After graduation and her chartered accountancy, she also acquired an MBA from Duke University and worked with Guidant Corp (USA) for six years before returning to India. Apart from Emcure, she runs Thapar Entreprneurs Academy that provides business education to young people (11 to 18 years). She has her own YouTube channel on women's health called Uncondition Yourself. She's also a published author. Namita has won several prestigious awards, like the 40 under Forty award by *Economic Times*, the Top 50 Most Powerful Women in Business award by *Business Today* and the Forbes Asia Power Business Women 2022 award. She's an avid movie fan, who named her sons Viru and Jai after the superhit *Sholay*.

LESSON I

The two Os

If there's ever an award for the most organized Shark, Namita will surely be the winner by miles. Her organizational skills help her manage time and resources effectively, which leads to increased productivity and efficiency. Being organized also helps her stay focused and reduces feelings of being overwhelmed by stress. She says it also helps her make better use of her time, which is divided between lots of things. 'My to-do lists help me prioritize tasks and focus on what is most important.'

While the organizational skills help her in prioritizing and delegating, and even maintaining a six-day workout schedule, her eternal optimism keeps Namita motivated and focused on long-term goals. 'Eternal optimism runs in my family. I remember my father experiencing losses year after year, being humiliated by many and asking my mother to tell creditors he wasn't at home when they called. All through this, he never lost his cool or his smile – a lesson in resilience and positivity,' she says.

Many business leaders like Namita swear by optimism as a quality – indeed, it's mentioned by the other Sharks as essential for an entrepreneur. Optimism can help you approach challenges with a positive attitude, leading to better problem-solving and decision-making. It can also help you to cope with stress and setbacks, since you believe things will work out in the end.

Optimism is also contagious, and it can help in creating a positive and supportive culture within your business. When you approach your work with a positive attitude, it inspires those around you to do the same, which leads to increased productivity and more collaboration.

Namita grew the India business from 500 crores to 2,000 crores and doubled the ebidta %. It is her ability to stay organized, always on top of things and her attention to detail that helps her manage 3,000 people and build large brands in women's health at Emcure.

Namita's father failed for 15 years before he succeeded in setting up a ₹7,000-crore business. 'I've seen his journey. The only thing that got him through was grit and how he looked at failures positively. **Rather than focusing on the hurt, focus on the learning.** You can't live your life in fear of failure,' she says.

Despite her punctuality, she's tolerant and good-humoured when those around her fail to meet the same standards – that might be due to the meditation practice. On one shoot, she turned up first (naturally!) and was then forced to hang around for many hours as the shoot was delayed. Instead of displaying normal signs of impatience, Namita spent her time writing a poem about the show, collating her experiences on the *Shark Tank* set. Once everyone was on set and ready to shoot, she made it a point to read it out to everyone.

SO WHAT DOES IT MEAN TO BE ORGANIZED?

How can you be organized? Let's break it up in different parts.

1. Planning and prioritization: Organized people are skilled at setting goals, creating plans and prioritizing tasks. If you're organized you can identify the most important tasks and focus on them first.
2. Attention to detail: Being detail-oriented is part of being organized.
3. Time management: Namita is a pro at managing time and balancing multiple tasks and commitments. She avoids wasting time on unnecessary/irrelevant activities.
4. Adaptability: Entrepreneurs must adapt quickly. Namita credits herself with being able to adapt quickly to changing circumstances, especially during the COVID-19 pandemic when the pharma industry was at the forefront of change. A good entrepreneur should be able to make adjustments to their plans, quickly if needed.
5. Self-discipline: This is probably one of the most underrated qualities of organized people. If you're self-disciplined, you can work independently and stay focused.

LESSON 2

Be both a shark and a dolphin

As you set up your business, you have to think about the problem you are solving, the size of market, investors, the consumer – but you shouldn't forget to work on your leadership style. Many founders are relatively inexperienced; there are a lot of things they have to learn, and learn fast. But you shouldn't forget yourself and your own journey as a leader of the business.

'A good leader is the one who can balance aggression and empathy,' says Namita.

She uses an extended metaphor in comparing leaders and their qualities to two iconic marine creatures – sharks and dolphins. She's even written an entire book around this theme!

Sharks are known for laser-focused ruthless aggression. Dolphins are known for their intelligence and cooperative pack-behaviour. The good leader must therefore, be both a shark and a dolphin. It's all about knowing when to become what.

'You have to know the right time to be firm and aggressive and show who the boss is, and the right time to show the empathy that your team may need. A leader needs to have both these traits and be able to balance both. Everyone has a shark and a dolphin within them. How well you balance the two really defines your success.'

In her book, *The Dolphin and The Shark*,[1] Namita writes that successful business leaders are often compared to sharks. The stereotypical tycoon or business leader is supposed to be ruthless, arrogant and aggressive. Weakness or vulnerability is looked down upon. However, in reality, successful leaders are also like dolphins – they are good team leaders who encourage cooperation and are empathetic to their team. 'A lot of those parameters are changing, especially post COVID-19,' she says.

Other Sharks agree. Peyush Bansal has built his leadership style around empathy, arguing that it's central to building a long-lasting business and that every entrepreneur needs to develop it in a 360-degree way. Vineeta Singh also says it's important to acknowledge your emotions – and how crying doesn't make her weak but allows her to de-stress.

When she was a child, Namita had very little self-confidence and believes this helped her develop empathy. As the eldest of nine grandkids in a traditional Gujarati joint family, she was expected to be a top-ranker in school. The entire discussion around her exams centred on the marks lost, rather than the marks gained. In addition, she was often teased for being overweight. 'These incidents built my character and made me more empathetic,' she says.

On *Shark Tank India*, there are times where she chooses to be very 'sharky' because honest feedback is needed and she also knows when to show love, kindness and care.

Empathy is an important trait for a leader. It allows you to understand and connect with the experiences and emotions of team members. It creates a positive and supportive work environment and will also help you make more informed decisions because you will understand how the team will respond.

In fact, Namita calls herself the 'Chief Problem-Solving Officer'. 'People just bring problems to me. I manage 3,000 people – sometimes there's an HR issue, sometimes marketing-related issues and sometimes people need to manage their own stress.' Having empathy has helped her be more approachable and open to feedback, and fostered a sense of trust and respect among her team.

This is also something every founder needs to work on. It can not only lead to better communication and collaboration within the team, it also helps you to better navigate conflicts and challenges that arise within the team.

THE USES OF OPTIMISM

Being an optimist helps in running any business for the following reasons.

1. Greater motivation: Being an optimist can increase your motivation and drive. You are more motivated to work hard, take risks and pursue your goals.

2. Increased resilience: Running a business can be challenging, and there will be setbacks and obstacles. Optimism helps you bounce back quickly.
3. Improved decision-making: If you're optimistic, you tend to have improved decision-making skills. You can see the bigger picture and focus on potential rewards, rather than dwelling on potential risks.
4. Enhanced leadership skills: Inspiring and motivating your team is one of the most essential qualities of a good leader. When you are optimistic and positive, you are more likely to create a positive work culture that encourages collaboration and creativity.

LESSON 3

Find a mentor, be a mentor

Like Peyush, Namita also has a few mentors who she turns to at various times. They act like her sounding boards, and she feels this is essential for running any start-up. She says that in our complex, stressful lives, we need someone with whom we can be our vulnerable selves. **'A mentor is not expected to know the answers and to tell you what to do but has the magical powers to ask the right questions that will lead you to your own insights and answers.'**

Namita had the good fortune of having three mentors at various stages in her life. Without mentioning names, she says, one of her mentors was on the board of Emcure and 'that made it easier to approach him'.

Her other two mentors are people she admired a lot but didn't know at first. 'Therefore, I cold called and requested they mentor me. Fortunately, both said yes,' she writes.

One of her mentors showed her that expectation management is key for a mentee. In Namita's case, for example, she believed that a mentor would always help her think through her business decisions, help her network with the right people and teach her important management lessons.

'One of my mentors showed me how wrong my expectations were.' He helped her understand that it was much more important to strengthen her core, to be in touch with her inner voice, to get rid of her ego and become a kinder, more authentic person. 'Once your core is strong, the rest will follow!'

After that learning, she replaced a long list of three-, five- and 10-year goals with timelines and milestones with two big life-goals – know yourself and help others.

What kind of mentor should you be looking for? Becoming a good start-up mentor requires a combination of knowledge, experience and skills. It's important to have a strong understanding of the start-up ecosystem and the various challenges and opportunities start-ups face. What you should be looking for are people with first-hand experience at building and growing successful businesses.

'A mentor is someone you deeply respect and want to emulate. Sometimes, it is a domain expert who can guide you. But a mentor need not be from the same industry. Rather, it has to be someone who can inspire you, give you brutally honest feedback sometimes and lift your spirits at other times,' she writes.[2]

Namita says that her mentors have played an important role in her life. 'They have helped me get better at my work through timely inputs on marketing, strategic calls I have had to make and even hiring decisions. They have been a sounding board when I have had emotionally trying moments at work, especially when I have had disagreements with my father. They have helped me evolve as a more authentic person by gently nudging me to be a better listener, to be less judgmental and, overall, a calmer person,' she notes in her book.[3]

Namita says that in an entrepreneur's journey, it helps to have successful founders as mentors as they can relate to the struggles and challenges faced. 'Their feedback could be more real, practical and contextual. They have your best interests at heart and will never judge or exploit your vulnerabilities.' She believes her mentors have made her a better person.

While it's important to find the right mentors, it's equally important for Namita to mentor others and to give back too. If you have experience as a start-up founder or have worked in a leadership role at a start-up, you may have valuable insights and expertise to share with founders. The key to being a good mentor involves being able to listen actively, ask thoughtful questions, give constructive feedback and help founders set and achieve their goals. She says that her biggest desire in life now is to mentor those who may need someone to guide and help them. 'Such is the chain of mentorship that what you receive you must generously give to others. That's the best payback for a good mentor.'

> ‘ It's not good for your mental health to constantly deal with challenges. The 3 Ms – massage, movies and meditation – help me to avoid reaching that breaking point. So I ensure that I schedule time for these on a routine basis. ’

LESSON 4

Make your teams as gender-balanced as possible

As you create your company, you'll have to think about what you want your team to look like. Namita strongly believes that everyone should have as much gender diversity in their teams as possible and that it can lead to better outcomes.

Women are good at multitasking; they tend not to overpromise and exaggerate. Their forecasts are often more grounded and they deliver more. Studies have shown that businesses with diverse leadership teams are more innovative and successful. This is why she has focused on mentoring women at work.

Yet women often face judgmental attitudes from their colleagues and employers: Will they come back after maternity leave? What happens if they get 'too attached' to the baby? Will mothers be able to put in long hours of work?

This discrimination shows itself in the world of start-ups too. Here's a shocking statistic: Just a little more than 1% (the exact number being 1.36%) of start-up funding in India in 2021 went to women (That's $900 million out of the total $42 billion raised that year).[4] But from JhaJi pickles to Thinkerbell, 49% of the start-ups that got funding in the first season of *Shark Tank India* had women co-founders. Having three women Sharks obviously made a difference.

Namita has spoken at length about her struggles as a working woman and her learnings from this. 'There are times I asked the questions in the meetings and men have looked at my father while answering them.' The discrimination never stopped.

Even after she got pregnant and asked for a flexible work schedule in the first year, she was labelled 'part-time' by many. 'The reality of senior women committed to their jobs is that regardless of time spent in the office, you are always working and never part-time!'

'There are challenges for women that need to be talked about. There are certain things holding them back, including they themselves. The more the number of women who break these stereotypes, the easier it'll be for the next generation of women entrepreneurs to emerge,' she says.

In *Shark Tank India* Season 1, Namita loved interacting with Rakhi Pal of Eventbeep who unapologetically said that she was okay with her family disowning her but she wouldn't give up on her dreams. She also mentions Jayanti Bhattacharya of India Hemp, who had responded sharply when Ashneer asked whether she was running her business as a hobby. Jayanti had retorted by asking if he was making this comment because she was a woman. Namita was the only Shark to defend her reaction and, later, the only one to make an offer as well.

Namita has five key lessons for women at work:

1. **Get rid of the guilt:** 'I often say that women are great at time management but terrible at guilt management. I feel it's a mental disorder that we need to work on. A simple example: When I miss my child's school event for a work commitment, I feel guilty. If I were to be a homemaker, I would have felt guilty about wasting my degrees. There's no right answer. Each to her own. Whatever your decision and your path, make peace with it and stop beating yourself up!'
2. **It's okay to be labelled selfish**: Women feel bad when they make time for themselves, their needs and their dreams. It's important to take this time to refresh and rejuvenate one's body and soul. If you take care of yourself and are happy, you will be a better mother, wife, daughter, employer and employee!
3. **Ask for help and not permission:** Women don't ask for help. They wonder what 'people might think' or 'they may find me incompetent'. But that's not the case. Everyone should ask for help whenever needed. You will be surprised how many well-meaning family members, friends and colleagues are happy to chip in. You don't need to be a perfectionist or superwoman.
4. **Learn to listen to your inner voice:** Trust your gut instinct. Take time to be in touch with your intuition, and like Steve Jobs said, 'Don't let the voice of others

drown your inner voice.'[5] This also means that once we learn to trust our inner voice as our biggest teacher, we must learn to ignore labels and stop seeking external validation.

5. **Don't limit yourself:** Women have a habit of blaming others, especially society. We create our own mental barriers and stop ourselves from reaching our true potential. Stop doing that. Dare to dream really big dreams.

How Namita invests

Being an entrepreneur herself helps in her investment journey, she feels. '**When you've been through setbacks, you can empathize with the challenges and the mindset of an entrepreneur. You know the mistakes you have made and what you learnt. I don't believe in being a passive investor. I believe in giving back and making an impact.'**

When investing in a start-up in *Shark Tank*, her decision is based on one of two things:

1. Unshakable facts, which means there have to be hard numbers and strong evidence that the start-up is investment-worthy and has the potential to scale up and be profitable in future.
2. In the absence of hard numbers, she goes with her

gut instinct. 'My instinct is my best teacher and it's something I listen to a lot,' she says.

She feels that there are a number of ways in which she, as an investor, can help start-ups. 'Investors have to provide business acumen in areas that are truly their expertise. This may involve help with marketing connects, hiring the right team depending on where current gaps are and help with distribution networks,' she says.

But sometimes there are conflicts with investors and the entrepreneur ultimately has to take the final call. The start-up Booz, for example, arrived in Season 1. Vineeta did not like the name while Ashneer Grover felt that it had good recall value. Similarly, for the energy drink start-up NOCD (no carbohydrate drink), the Sharks felt that the name was tough to pronounce and the entrepreneurs agreed to a name change, since the start-up was in its early stages.

She feels **there's a thin line between success and failure for a long-term investor**. Some investors give the founder the freedom and flexibility to do what they feel is truly right and that might make the critical difference. '**The investor must always be someone who supports and empowers rather than someone who bogs entrepreneurs down with too many demands and dashboards,**' she writes in her book.[6]

NAMITA'S GUIDE TO STARTING A START-UP

- Think of yourself as a shark and a dolphin – be both aggressive and empathetic.
- Find mentors – but also mentor others.
- Cultivate the two Os – optimism and organization – and the world is your oyster.
- Always know your numbers.
- Focus on customer insights.
- Be a lifelong learner.

5

Anupam Mittal's Winning Hand: Using Poker Skills to Dominate His Investment Game

'Just like in poker, in real-time investing you need to read the room. You have to read the other players. In poker there's a big fallacy that you're playing cards. You're playing people, the cards just happen to be there. Same thing in early-stage investing. You are fundamentally trying to understand people.'

Picture a poker player sitting calmly at the card table next to a stack of chips. His face is a mask of concentration. His eyes flicker back and forth between his cards and the faces of the other players, taking in every subtle cue and expression. He maintains a steady, emotionless expression, revealing nothing about the strength or weakness of the hand.

Poker players use a variety of tricks to throw off their opponents. They'll sometimes casually glance at their chips when they have a strong hand, making it appear as if they're considering a big bet. They masterfully employ the art of bluffing, making bold bets with weak hands to intimidate opponents into folding.

They also meticulously observe their opponents' betting patterns and tendencies, taking mental notes of how they react in different situations. They know who is tight, and who is loose with their betting and money management, as well as who is more likely to bluff.

The game of investing is rather similar to the game of poker. Anupam Mittal says, 'Poker is all about reading the room, reading the other players and taking a bet; that's what we do as investors, especially on *Shark Tank*.'

Just like in poker, Anupam the investor is fully immersed in the game – his mind always working overtime to judge start-up founders, trying to stay ahead in the hunt of a good deal. His confidence and control while running his businesses, and as a Shark on *Shark Tank India*, make him a force to be reckoned with.

Anupam returned several times to the game of poker when he was looking for ways to describe the investor and founder mindsets. There is, however, a key difference between poker and investing.

Poker is a zero-sum game where one player's gains equate to the others' losses. In contrast, investing is a win-win game, where the investor puts up cash that helps an entrepreneur run a business for profits and both benefit. Yet while the investor and the entrepreneur are on the same side, they are also bargaining for larger slices of the business. The investor asks for a larger stake for a smaller contribution and the founder tries to offer as little stake as possible while getting the maximum funding. In this sense, just like poker, there is often a battle of a kind between the investor and the entrepreneur.

Of all the Sharks, Anupam has been a serial investor, having invested in over 250 companies. Thus he is not just a successful entrepreneur but also truly understands what drives investors.

WHO IS ANUPAM MITTAL?

Anupam Mittal is an Indian entrepreneur and angel investor best known for running the matchmaking platform Shaadi.com and the real-estate platform Makaan.com. He also founded the short video application Mauj and the media company Mobango. His parent company People Group also produces Bollywood movies and has invested in over 250 start-ups, primarily in tech companies, including Ola, Rupeek, Rapido, Chalo, Jupiter, Porter, etc.

He graduated from Boston College in 1997 and lived in America for almost 10 years before he decided to return to India. Back in 2001, as the dot-com bubble burst, he launched a start-up in India.

LESSON I

Take risks

Anupam is always willing to take risks. He launched his start-up at the height of the dot-com crisis, for example. He says, 'some part of it has to do with my family background. I come from an entrepreneurial family. My father had to take on economic responsibilities when he was only 13 years old. My grandfather died and he had to take care of three brothers and four sisters. He was the sole breadwinner and so took up a job as a clerk that paid him ₹100 per month.'

Mittal senior worked his way up, building his own businesses and that only happened because he was willing to take risks. As his son says, 'He could have very well concentrated on being promoted while working a job. Watching him taking risks and being an entrepreneur through my formative years created an entrepreneurial streak in me. You could add another thing – my need to explore. That comes from my mom. She has a deep sense of adventure that perpetually remains unfulfilled.'

In her seventies, his mother has taught herself to use social media and email, published three books and written hundreds of poems; she's now working with Adivasis to help them build a better life. 'She has that spirit. If you take the entrepreneurial streak from my dad and combine it with a sense of exploration from my mom, that's the combination that makes me.'

The ability to take risks is at the heart of any entrepreneurial activity. Risk-taking is built into Anupam's DNA. It may not be for you. But if you don't have an appetite for taking a chance, then launching a start-up may not be for you. Every Shark, and most founders, had to take a leap into the unknown and stake everything to make things work. So will you.

> ‘I have become poorer after *Shark Tank*. Whenever I ask for the price of something, the shopkeeper quotes me a higher price.’

LESSON 2

Embrace the struggle, not failure

‘It is fashionable to say failure leads to success – it's a stepping stone. If you look hard enough it's only successful people who say that. It's easy to say that once you become a success. But failure is miserable. It can become very toxic. For every failure that turned into a success, there are a thousand failures that got very toxic,' says Anupam.

He's had his fair share of frustrating times. ‘I've been penniless twice in my life after seeing a certain amount of success. After being a multi-millionaire, being broke and in debt is very hard. I punished myself a lot for it.'

‘So, instead of saying enjoy the failure, I say embrace the struggle. That's a moving goal and a moving target. Once you realize life is a struggle, you start taking victories and losses in your stride. Treat life as a game, just like poker,' he says.

> ‘As a businessman you must stay grounded, that makes you a better businessman and also a better human being.’

LESSON 3

Panic creatively

The founder of any business has to handle a huge amount of pressure. Vineeta cries to let off steam; in the chapter, 'Lessons from *Shark Tank*', we will hear a story from a founder about when the pressure got too high. Anupam sees it a little differently. While suffering from anxiety and depression has to be dealt with, he believes that extreme tension can also lead to creativity, what he calls the 'incredible power that comes with that panic'.

Anupam freely admits that he has had mental health issues – he deals with something called generalized anxiety disorder. This means he's often on the edge of a panic attack.

He says **panic lends him the 'ability to think creatively and laterally**. To cut across different disciplines and apply your knowledge laterally in real time and merge various concepts – that power is my boon and my bane. That is my superpower if you will, when I can think very creatively at very high speeds, such as in conceiving iconic ad campaigns.'

'Mental strength comes from dealing with high-stress situations, and the connection with anti-fragility – not getting overwhelmed by any situation – is interesting.

Put me in any situation and I can figure my way out. It comes from my fragility. The only way to gain composure and mental strength is to be constantly fragile, constantly flirting with being close to choking but managing to come out of it. You have to be fragile to become anti-fragile.'

He confesses to having choked on stage to the point where he couldn't speak. And he knows he carries the risk of choking again, every time he's due to speak. 'If you want to go from fragility to anti-fragile there is no 100% guarantee. But you can become fragile-resistant by putting yourself in the deep end.'

> 'As we become entrepreneurs, you get locked up in your ivory towers, you lose touch with the average person on the street who are the exact people you started your business for. The further you get away from reality, the closer your demise is.'

LESSON 4

Be naive, be delusional

There's a lot of power in delusion when you're starting out as an entrepreneur, Anupam says. '**You have to be delusional since the chances of you succeeding are so thin that if you're not delusional, you'll take up a safe job.**

It's like becoming an actor – there's little chance you'll become a star.'

Mittal says founders need a certain amount of deep conviction. 'A healthy level of naivety early on is extremely important for you to keep going. If you do not have that foolishness, lot of successful people will not be successful, including myself. I deluded myself for years. That conviction may not be based in reality; it is based on self-belief.'

Returning to the poker analogy, Anupam says, 'When you first start playing poker, you fail a couple of times and then you start to play the real game. Delusion is replaced by genuine self-confidence only when you get a few victories. You start understanding when you win, why you win. There is no other way.'

> 'When it comes to business, building long-term value, creating something institutional, leaving a mark or creating a benchmark, substance is eternal.'

LESSON 5

Profit or growth?

The right way to run a business is to be long-term greedy instead of optimizing for the short-term. Anupam gives the example of four great football legends – Pelé, Maradona, Messi and Mbappé. 'Their lives unfolded very differently but the journey of becoming a legend was very similar. They each put in 25 years of hard work to become stars. Even though we are talking about players of different generations, with different styles and different characters. I think it's the same for business.'

Principles in business don't change, core philosophies of business don't change. 'Revenue is vanity, profit is sanity, cash is king. These are **the foundations that matter – growth, market-share and profits.** You can go back to any earlier generation and it will be the same.'

However, while that's Anupam's approach, the start-up industry has typically chased growth at any cost. Which way will you go? Anupam says you won't be able to make this decision alone and that the type of business you're in will determine whether you chase growth or profitability. If you're in a winner-takes-all industry, and there are two to three other competitors that have already raised significant capital and have a loss-driven growth model, you either have to exit the market, or you'll have to play the same game. You don't have a choice.

In addition, it's important to reflect who you are as a person and what you are comfortable doing. If you thrive in bull markets with competitive intensity, and raising capital, growing and driving market share comes naturally to you, then that's what you should be doing.

Certain industries have very powerful network effects, especially the consumer tech industry where margins are very high and if you emerge amongst the top two players. So if you're that sort of business, you should always choose growth. Otherwise you will not survive.

LESSON 6

Success means survival

The fundamental job of an entrepreneur is to make sure you survive year after year. If you keep doing that for 15 years, suddenly you'll discover you're an overnight success. How do you keep on going?

A rulebook has emerged about how to be innovative: create proof of concept, test it; fail fast, fail forward; build a prototype and set elements of design; create a feedback loop. Many of these things have now developed.

This cycle encourages failure. Anupam has been through this mill many times, both as an entrepreneur and as an investor.

'I stumbled, I fell, picked myself up again, licked my wounds, went on again. The No. 1 rule of entrepreneurship is that you've to show up on the battlefield every day. There will be days and months when you'll fail. But you still have to show up.' That's the first rule of survival.

Another reason why start-ups fail is that founders fall out with each other. Anupam's advice for entrepreneurs is to 'take half a day on Saturday. Just co-founders. Talk about all the big stuff. Anybody who says anything about operations has to pay ₹10,000. Talk about the following: Do you have product-market fit? How much runway do we have? Do we need more capital? What are we not seeing? Long-term strategy? What's the competition doing?'

A third reason is that start-ups don't adapt quickly enough, or they think they can raise more money and spend their way out of trouble. **It's not the strongest who wins, it's really the most adaptive.**

Or they didn't find product-market fit. But by the time they realize it, it's too late.

> 'Call me a late bloomer but I think my journey has only started. My entire journey up to here is not my achievement, it's a foundational course, and what I'll do now and in the future will be my actual achievements.'

LESSON 7

The Indian way of doing business

There's an exceptionalism to doing business in India. 'We're a land of tribes, not a single homogeneous population.'

As Anupam points out, in America, the fundamental responsibility of communication lies with the speaker; in India, it lies with the listener. 'Indians will say "understood", but you're saying something else. We play Chinese whispers and it leads to loss of productivity. I was extremely frustrated when I first came back. I had a habit of saying, "Summarize. What did you take away?"

The other big difference according to him is that trust doesn't come easily. India is a low-trust society.

'I never had to read between the lines in the US, whereas business conversation in India is very politically heavy and nuanced.'

LESSON 8

How Anupam invests

Anupam is the ultimate investor – he has invested in over 250 companies. 'Am I a kingmaker or a king? I have founded many companies and invested in many more successfully. But while people associate kings with aggressive A-type personalities that outshout each other,

I think that's the wrong definition. To me a king is somebody who doesn't need to prove he's a king. Your presence, your aura, your experience, your wisdom is enough. If you have to beat your chest and announce the king is here, you're far, far away from being a king.'

Anupam's father once told him, 'The day I stop working is the day I die.' He sees that as a cornerstone of his life's philosophy. As a supporter of entrepreneurship, he believes that India's destiny will change when global-scale desi entrepreneurs appear.

He believes his way of giving back is to 'create a lot of entrepreneurs and, if I can, to help other people do that. Look at the world. There are no kings anymore; you have leaders. You can be a strong leader and create other strong leaders.'

Many of the companies he has invested in, have become hugely successful. Over 12 years, he claims 46% realized internal rate of return (IRR) in early-stage investing.

Anupam stays ahead by reading a lot, constantly talking to entrepreneurs and, most importantly, observing a lot. 'Success at investing only happens when you spend a lot of time researching it. I don't have the patience for conventional research. But I could draw upon other disciplines and in real time process the available information and ask the questions that matter. That's served me very well in my investing career.'

How Anupam decides on his investments

Like all investors, Anupam looks at the **opportunity** of any business by assessing the potential market, and technology trends. He also judges the business on likely timeframes and what other investors and competitors may be doing.

However, ultimately, he bets on the person. Here he relies heavily on instinct and evaluating the person. What is the body language? What are the words they say and how do they say them? 'There are a lot of tell-tale signs, just like in poker. I'm looking for a twitch in trying to understand that person. Especially on *Shark Tank*, I don't have time to deeply analyse and decide, and that's when the poker analogy really makes sense.'

Pedigree to Anupam is evidence that you've done something exceptional in life. That could be IIT/IIM but it doesn't have to be. It could also mean you climbed Mt Everest, or you became a top athlete, or a top social media influencer. Anupam wants some evidence of exceptionalism.

'Most of them are going to fail. But **if I want to bet my hard-earned money, I'm going to bet on exceptional people. To me, that's what pedigree is.** I bet on people who have proved they are exceptional or who I believe are going to do something exceptional.'

Also, he looks for business acumen. 'You must have a

commercial instinct. Great product builders are not great business builders. People often confuse that.'

Another useful quality is perseverance. 'It takes 10 to 20 years to build an amazing company in India and to create a lot of value. Poker tournaments are very tiring and go on for days and days. You have to have stamina to persevere, and in business you need to persevere for the next 10 years. I have to judge if you have that capacity and the hunger to win. **You should be so hungry that you can't bear the thought of a competitor. If you think of a competitor, you just find a way to eliminate them.**'

He's prepared to be contrarian and not be part of the crowd when it comes to his picks. He cites VCs and PEs who can't afford to sit out a trend, whether it's crypto or electric vehicles. Errors of omission, he points out, are much worse than errors of commission. **Pick the wrong business, you lose some money – but if you miss out on picking the big winner, you've actually lost a lot more.**

This FOMO leads to a lot of people chasing a few dreams and creates bubbles and boom-bust cycles.

'We try not to do that as an investor. I try to take a counterview. It doesn't always work, I make mistakes. But we try not to get caught in the wave,' says Anupam.

If things go bad, people will say 'I told you so', but as Anupam says, 'Everyone would love to have crazy growth with crazy profitability. But unfortunately, that's not how the world works.'

ANUPAM'S GUIDE TO STARTING A START-UP

- Be audacious! It's often easier working on seemingly impossible projects than playing the same game as others.
- Don't optimize for the short-term; be long-term greedy.
- Building a valuable start-up takes a long time, so find an area you are passionate about.
- If there is one trait to build a culture around, it's the ability to constantly question the status quo.
- Build your entire business around technology because managing people is very, very expensive.

6

Fail Fast, Learn Faster Like Amit Jain

‘You can’t take too much time in learning and overplanning; your agility and nimbleness will suffer. It is better to be an executionist rather than a strategist.’

Once upon a time there was an IT professional who left the small town of Jaipur to make it big with his fancy degrees and high-paying jobs. He was constantly on the move: juggling work, long commutes and a busy social life first in the US' Texas and later in India's Silicon Valley, Bengaluru. Soon after, he started missing the simplicity and peace he had grown up with in Jaipur. The constant noise and chaos of city life left him feeling stressed and disconnected. He longed for the closeness of his family, the home-cooked meals and the culture he had grown up around. The sense of community that he had left behind burned a huge hole in his heart. City life, in a way, left him feeling lonely and isolated, while he missed the warmth and togetherness that his joint family once provided. This is probably why he couldn't resist when the love of his family called out to him and he decided to move back. The family's love and support, he says, not only brought him back home but also, eventually, helped him find success and fulfillment. This is the story of Amit Jain, an entrepreneur who dared to build an IT business in a small city like Jaipur, where 'startup culture' was unheard of at that time.

Cut to 2008, the genesis of CarDekho. It started with a feeling of deep frustration when Amit Jain was walking through the Auto Expo – India's largest auto show – and he wanted more information on some of the cars that wowed him. Surfing after he returned home, he discovered there wasn't a single website which listed the detailed features, specifications and price comparisons he was interested in.

That sparked an idea. Amit created an online database aggregating information and data from the physical brochures he had picked up at the expo. CarDekho actually started more like an experiment that fulfilled Amit's need to build a business, sitting in his hometown. Later, he discovered that like him, there were many people looking to research cars online, which meant both ad revenues and potential conversions into actual vehicle sales for a website that fulfilled their searches. And the result was a traffic explosion that converted into unimaginable revenues!

Amit realized that he had stumbled upon a gap in the automobile market. That was the beginning of CarDekho, one of India's largest online car portals. The website generates 88% organic traffic and has over 62 million monthly active users. It caters to 90% of new car buyers researching on their platform. In fact, it contributes to almost 30% of sales of India's automakers it works with on their sale model.[1] The group handles transactions worth $2 billion (Q3 FY23

ARR basis) and has registered a compound annual growth rate (CAGR) of 70% over a period of last 10 years in revenue.[2] CarDekho group's FY22 consolidated operating revenue has grown by 81% (year-over-year growth, or YOY) to ₹1,600 crores.[3] It has unicorn status based on the most recent valuations and is angling for an IPO in FY23.

Additionally, InsuranceDekho, the insurance arm of the CarDekho group, is the No.1 B2B2C player in insurtech, where they issue nearly 2 lakh auto insurance policies per month through their 80,000 agents who are active across 98% of pin codes in India. CarDekho is also a market leader with a 14% market share in the used car finance market – they disburse nearly 10,000 used car loans amounting to ₹700 crore per month through their platform called RuPay. The group also has a presence in South East Asia and has a market share of nearly 7% in the used car finance market in Indonesia.

'I never thought it'll be so big. For me, setting it up was more circumstantial – my brother and I had to move back to our hometown (Jaipur) to take care of our father who was diagnosed with cancer in 2005. We were looking to move back and start a company in Jaipur since there was no IT industry there at that time,' Amit says.

This was in 2006. A year later, in 2007, Amit and his brother Anurag had launched GirnarSoft, an IT consultancy firm. It was a stereotypical IT start-up – the duo worked out of their garage just like the founders of

Amazon, Apple, Microsoft, Google had done in their early days. The business started flourishing and from a garage office, they moved to a full-fledged one in 2008. By the next year, GirnarSoft went bust, and the brothers had to rebuild the company again. The experience taught Amit a valuable lesson: there's no such thing as quick success. **'I started investing in the stock market to make a quick buck but such a thing doesn't exist.** In hindsight, you're always a better version of yourself,' he says.

WHO IS AMIT JAIN?

Amit Jain is the 46-year-old CEO of GirnarSoft – his brother and co-founder Anurag is the COO while his wife Pihu is the director for their CSR project in Girnar Foundation. CarDekho is the flagship portal of the company. Hailing from Jaipur, Amit graduated from IIT Delhi. Prior to launching the start-up, Amit had worked at Tata Consultancy Services and Trilogy (in Austin, Texas) for several years, before starting the CarDekho group, which today is India's leading autotech ecosystem player building consumer-centric solutions in the journey of owning the mobility. With platforms like CarDekho, BikeDekho, InsuranceDekho, RuPay, ZigWheels, PowerDrift, etc., Amit and his brother Anurag host more than 62 million monthly active users. The company is expanding rapidly in South East Asian markets and has operations in four countries. Amit Jain became a Shark in Season 2 of *Shark Tank India*.

LESSON I

Fail fast, learn faster

Amit was an IIT graduate who started working in the US in 2000. The reason for leaving just after a year was a philosophical one. He didn't take well to the individualistic nature of the American society. He recalls showing up at an NRI friend's house one day only to be asked, 'Have I called upon you?'. This is not how friends back home treated each other, he remembers thinking to himself. Around the same time he returned to India to set-up Trilogy's Bengaluru office. The thought of going back was always at the back of his mind, but the trigger point didn't come until 2005 when his father was diagnosed with cancer. In 2006, when he passed away, the writing was on the wall. 'It was between my entire family shifting their base to Bengaluru or me moving back. My brother and I chose the latter. This kind of love of the joint family gets you back,' he says. Their father was a gemstone trader. After his death, for the first six months, the brothers tried their hand at running the gemstone trading business. But that was not where they were finding their spark and it wasn't intellectually stimulating. 'It was a very humbling experience to move around on the streets of different cities with our jholas hoping to strike a good deal and meet potential clients,' Amit says. Later, they decided to start an IT outsourcing company because they were good at coding.

At first, things at GirnarSoft were going well. The Jain brothers soon hired a team of 20 people for their IT outsourcing firm. It was only after a year of operations and turning profitable that they moved to conventional offices. But then disaster struck and it was largely the brothers' fault.

GirnarSoft went bankrupt when the stock market crashed in 2009. The Jain brothers had invested close to ₹1.5 crore in stock-trading and the whole amount was wiped out in five days. 'We were betting at 10x leverage (meaning they had positions worth ₹15 crore). But Sensex fell from 18,000 to 6,000. This is something that nobody could ever have imagined. But as an entrepreneur, if you fall down, you get back up again,' he says.

That early-stage learning was very important for him. '**Every failure forces a better version out of you**,' he says. 'Very few people have the ability to absorb failure. Persistence is what defines a good founder.'

Starting and growing a business can be a challenging and difficult process. There will be setbacks and failures along the way, and it can be easy to become discouraged or lose motivation. However, persistence allows a founder to stay focused and keep moving, even when faced with obstacles or setbacks. It helps a founder stay committed to their vision when things get tough.

That's exactly what Amit did. At the time, they had 70 to 80 employees and they had to take loans to pay salaries. The company was back on its feet in less than a year and the brothers swore to never dabble in stock trading ever again. This taught them to treat money with respect and Amit learnt never to casually use money from the corporate account for such risky punts.

Amit had to use the same agility when he launched CarDekho. '**Daily you do something new and fail and try to learn quickly from your mistakes**. We started opening different verticals depending on what the customers' feedback suggested they wanted us to enter in.'

Early on, Amit had tried to sell mobiles online a few months after he started CarDekho and got high traffic. But he realized that there were big challenges. Phones got stolen and disappeared between warehouse and customer. Plus, there were bigger players giving discounts.

'We soon understood that we can neither give those kinds of discounts (because we had no money), nor can we deal with the challenges of running a phone-selling platform online. It didn't take too much time for us to understand that it was time to pivot. We quickly launched pricedekho.com and started offering price comparison across platforms. We made it into an aggregator marketplace instead of directly selling phones online,' Amit explains.

> ‘Once you go to IIT–IIM, you're perceived as the crème. But in the long run it's a disadvantage because as soon as an IIT–IIM student graduates, they can join a cushy job. After that education and those job titles, you don't have the risk-taking appetite left. Of course, there are outliers.’

LESSON 2

Speed counts

Amit and his brother's original plan was to develop GirnarSoft. However, they quickly realized that this was not an easily scalable business. Around this time they went to the Auto Expo and had their idea. 'We picked up all the brochures and coded a site within seven days,' he says.

CarDekho got instant traffic and they pivoted the IT consulting business towards the auto sector. Within three years, in 2011, they had become 'the market leader in traffic. At that time our monthly ad revenue was ₹40–50 lakh from just Google ads. Then Autotrader (an $8 billion company back then) wanted to do a deal and invited us to Atlanta for three days. That opened up our vision. Till then, we only knew that we had great traffic but now we could see what can be built on the backend of an online information aggregation portal.

Then we looked for funding because we needed money to build. **Always raise money to scale, not to survive.** That's my advice for founders. We raised $15 million in the first round. CarDekho has raised close to $500 million so far in multiple rounds of funding.

By being aggressive and taking decisive action, a start-up can move quickly to seize opportunities and establish itself in the market and by aggressively pursuing new customers and partnerships, a start-up can quickly increase its market share.

'Being aggressive in the early stages of a start-up can help a company secure a first-mover advantage and gain visibility and attention in the market, which can be important for attracting investment, partnerships and customers,' Amit says. 'Being aggressive can also help a start-up stay competitive and ahead of its rivals, which can be crucial for its long-term success.'

LESSON 3

Target consumers not cars

Amit says he still hadn't grasped just how much potential the new website possessed. But after a few Google searches and some analysis of growing web traffic, he was pretty sure of what he wanted to do.

'I realized the potential of online businesses. That is

when I understood that we didn't want to make a business about cars but about consumers,' he says. 'You build a company based on what the customer imagines you to be. When consumers want insurance, we built a portal for that. When consumers wanted financing, we added another portal and of course, if they wanted to sell their car, we had to add the next vertical dealing with second-hand cars.'

The group decided on a house of brands strategy. It would provide for consumer needs, centred on the personal transport market. The different portals would mostly run under the distinctive 'Dekho' branding. Now, GirnarSoft runs multiple brands, such as CarDekho, BikeDekho, InsuranceDekho, Rupyy, Zigwheels, etc.

A 'house of brands' strategy creates, markets and sells multiple brands, though each segment operates independently and has its own unique identity, product line and target market. The company acts like a parent or umbrella organization, managing overall strategy for the various brands, but allowing each brand to retain its own distinct personality and branding.

A house of brands can offer a diverse range of products and services and can appeal to a wide variety of consumers. Virgin would be the most famous example, perhaps, but many multinationals have successfully used this strategy.

There are several advantages to using a house of brands

strategy rather than creating individual brands for every distinct products.

Diversification: The umbrella allows a company to offer a wide range of products and services to different target markets while sharing the same brand associations. This reduces advertising costs and the success of one product enhances the credibility of the next product with the same branding. (Note: The opposite is also true – if one product suffers loss of credibility, so do others with the same brand!)

Brand loyalty: Each brand within a house of brands can build its own loyal customer base, which can lead to increased customer retention and brand loyalty.

Brand differentiation: Even within a house of brands, every brand can build its own unique identity and positioning, which helps to differentiate the products in the market.

Resource sharing: A house of brands can share resources such as distribution, advertising and marketing across its brands, which helps to reduce costs and improve efficiency.

Customer insights: A house of brands can provide valuable customer insights and data from its various brands, which helps inform strategy and decision-making.

Amit's strategy has included growing inorganically by acquiring competitors like Gaadi.com and ZigWheels. After realizing the reach of his own business, he explored the potential for similar verticals. GirnarSoft started portals like BikeDekho, BusesDekho, BatteryDekho, InsuranceDekho, which collectively draw over 55 million unique visitors per month.

But every expansion has to be accompanied by a simple question – why should I do this and how will it help the customer? 'You make a team, you look at expansion. Then you look at adjacent categories or vertical expansion **but one thing should be clear – that you are solving for a very important consumer need,**' he says.

LESSON 5

Look for white space

'White space' refers to untapped market opportunities or areas where there is little or no competition. Identifying and exploiting white space can be a powerful way for a start-up to differentiate itself and gain a foothold in a crowded market. It happened almost accidentally with Amit, for example, when he discovered that there were no online resources to check for details on cars and, upon further investigation, that online resources were lacking for a host of automobile-related services. There were similar portals abroad but in India CarDekho was one of the first.

To find white space, you'll need to do some research and analysis to identify areas where there is a need or demand for a product or service that is not being met. This might involve looking at trends in the market, analysing customer needs or identifying gaps in the offerings of existing competitors.

Once you've identified a potential white space, you'll need to assess whether it is a viable opportunity for your start-up. This will involve evaluating factors such as the size of the market, the potential for growth, and the resources and expertise required to enter the market. If you're able to identify and successfully exploit a white space, it can provide a unique advantage for your start-up and help you stand out in a crowded market.

'A big company generally doesn't focus on white space because either it's too small or it's not a tried-and-tested market. That's what a start-up founder needs to tap,' Amit says.

> ‘The customer will tell you what's working, you just need to constantly be in touch with them. You need to find a white space in either the products or the pricing or experience.’

LESSON 6

Create a plan – but don't overthink it

A well-thought-out business plan can help a start-up better understand its market, target customers and competition. It also helps in clarifying its goals and priorities, which can improve its focus and help it to allocate resources effectively.

While seeking investments, a comprehensive and professional business plan is a key component in convincing venture capitalists or angel investors to bet on the company and its future growth trajectory.

'Planning can help a start-up anticipate challenges and opportunities and make more informed and strategic decisions about its business. It can help align the goals and efforts of a start-up's team members, which can improve communication and collaboration within the organization,' he says. One can also optimize their own operations and processes, which can improve efficiency and reduce waste for the company.

But planning only takes you so far. Amit never really planned for this scale when he first launched the auto-portal. And, in fact, he hates overplanning. **'You can't take too much time learning things; your agility will suffer. If you overplan, your nimbleness will suffer. Be an executionist, not a strategist,'** he says.

Start-up founders often find planning time-consuming.

Developing a comprehensive business plan can divert resources and attention away from product development or customer acquisition.

A business plan can prove very helpful in outlining a company's goals and strategies. But the market and industry in which a start-up operates may be highly dynamic and change rapidly. As a result, a business plan that is too rigid may not be able to adapt.

Another downside of having an elaborate plan is unrealistic expectations. It is natural for a start-up to be optimistic about its potential for success, but this optimism shouldn't lead to unrealistic expectations and assumptions.

> ‘ In order to be a founder, you need to be frugal. When you're in a job, you fly business class and stay at the best hotels, but it's different when you spend your own money. ’

LESSON 7

Bootstrap up

Amit knows all about handling small, underfunded start-ups thanks to that early experience. Founders have to wear many hats in order to get such businesses rolling. 'They may be responsible for everything from product development and marketing to sales and customer service. Starting a business from a garage can be challenging, but it can also be a very rewarding experience,' he says. Like many other successful entrepreneurs, he credits the early struggles and challenges for building resilience and determination.

'When you're bootstrapped, you're the salesman, you're the developer. Running a bootstrapped company is a challenging but rewarding experience.'

The most important part is to focus on a specific niche. 'It's easier to start and grow a business when you have a clear target market in mind.' By focusing on a specific niche, one can better understand the needs and wants of your customers and tailor your products or services accordingly,' Amit says.

As a bootstrapped company, it's important to be mindful of costs. Keep your overheads as low as possible. This helps stretch resources and gives companies the flexibility to reinvest profits back into the business. 'As a small bootstrapped company, you have the advantage of being able to move quickly and pivot as needed. Stay attuned to market trends and be willing to adapt your business model as needed to stay competitive,' Amit says.

> ' A business is built twice: once it's built in the mind, then it's built in real. People need to dream big. '

How Amit invests

The Shark who debuted in *Shark Tank India* Season 2 says that it was the first time he turned into an angel investor. Amit bets on founders trying to solve a problem rather than just asking for investment because it's a fad.

Investment, he adds, is an outcome when one builds a business for themselves. 'It's not a milestone to be celebrated.'

He says that founders need to be very clear why they want to start their own companies.

Many entrepreneurs are driven by a desire to solve a problem or fill a gap in the market. They see an opportunity to create a product or service that addresses a need or pain point. It allows them to be their own boss, pursue their passions and have a greater sense of control.

Of course, one of the main motivations for starting a company is financial gain. But Amit says that entrepreneurs driven by the desire to create something new and innovative are more long-lasting. 'They want to bring a fresh perspective or solution to the market and make a positive impact on the world. **If you're happy with the journey, you'll make it big. It shouldn't be for the heck of it.**'

All said and done, he still doesn't feel he's arrived. 'As a start-up founder, it's impossible to feel you've arrived. **If you start feeling you've arrived, you lose the vision of going forward. You have to constantly be hungry,**' he says.

According to Amit, investors bet on two things: whether the market can be big and whether the founder and his team can be trusted. **'One should never go for funding when it's about survival but when there's a need to scale the company, a vision to expand and build a brand,'** he says.

Experience can certainly be helpful in starting and running a start-up, as it can provide valuable insights, skills and knowledge that can help increase the chances of success. However, it's important to note that experience is not a requirement for running or starting a successful start-up. Many successful entrepreneurs have started their businesses with little or no experience in that specific industry. It's the attitude and hunger that count.

AMIT'S GUIDE TO STARTING A START-UP

- Be quick – fail, learn, try something else. Just keep going as fast as possible.
- Try to fundraise for scale, not for survival.
- Find a niche to create a business – or a white space, as Amit calls it.
- Be careful and responsible about your company's money.
- Focus on execution, don't overthink or overplan.

7

Lessons from *Shark Tank India*

By now, you have hopefully learnt more about the Sharks, how they have achieved what they have, and what it takes in the way of emotional balance, leadership and management skill to take a start-up from just an idea to a successful business. Hopefully, too, the book will have taught you another invaluable lesson – what it takes to pitch to an investor and win them over.

But remember, what you see on the show is a heavily edited version of the actual Q&A session and presentation. Sharks ask a lot of questions, many of which are edited out of the 10 minutes or so that every pitch receives onscreen. Some of this is dropped purely for reasons of time but a lot of it consists of 'boring' data – numbers and projections that the founders make, which are analysed in detail by the Sharks. So the pitch you make has to be deeper and better researched than the slightly superficial versions you see onscreen. You must be prepared for awkward questions and 'deep drilling'.

The Sharks were chosen for their different personalities and they operate across a broad spectrum of different sectors. The show also makes it clear that they think differently in many ways. They've heard all sorts of pitches, and different Sharks have pitched in with offers for different types of start-ups. In the two seasons, only one business received an offer from all six Sharks.

But there are certain common qualities all the Sharks seem to look for, no matter the line of business. While they favour different types of businesses as individuals, they are all extremely interested in the personalities of the founders.

Here's what they are looking for:

1. Optimists – The Sharks all agree that optimists are better-suited temperamentally to run start-ups, which are bound to go through ups and downs.
2. Empathy – Empathetic people make better team-leaders.
3. Honesty – If you are detailing past revenues and making future projections, the hard numbers should be as honest and credible as possible.
4. Flexibility – A founder must know when to pivot if something is not working.
5. Pushiness when it comes to marketing and developing the business – what is described as 'shamelessness'.
6. Confidence – If you can't project success, it won't happen.
7. Founders who can seek advice and find mentors.

8. And while you can't change your personality, you can 'fake it till you make it', and cultivate confidence, optimism and empathy.

So now, let's look at a few of the entrepreneurs who hit the jackpot, and one who decided to reboot and shut down his business despite receiving an endorsement from the Sharks.

Pratik Gadia: Stitching things together

Pratik Gadia, founder and CEO, Yarn Bazaar, has a vision – to organize the unorganized textile industry. He says, 'Our aim is to create an end-to-end yarn platform serving all needs and pain points of the industry; making it very seamless and efficient.' Yarn Bazaar is a holistic B2B yarn marketplace, which targets solving the problem of broken supply chains in the traditional textile industry.

Pratik featured on the first season of *Shark Tank India*, and his company raised ₹1 crore from Peyush Bansal, Ashneer Grover, Aman Gupta and Anupam Mittal. After watching the show, one of the biggest global manufacturers, H&M, reached out to him for help.

Pratik was born and brought up in textile manufacturing and distribution, since that was his family's business. When his father was just 15, he ran away from his village in Jhunjhunu District, Rajasthan, to avoid studying. Gadia senior went to Nepal and joined a small company as a saree salesman. That was his entry into textiles. He later shifted to Kolkata as a commission agent in the late eighties and eventually moved to Mumbai in the early nineties and entered manufacturing for a few clients in Delhi and Kolkata.

This story from a bygone era is a great example of how entrepreneurship is hardly an alien concept in India. Long before the word 'start-up' was coined and shows like *Shark Tank* were dreamt of, millions of wannabe Indian entrepreneurs dreamt of building their own businesses.

After completing his bachelor's in Bombay, Pratik joined the family business with the typical gung-ho attitude of a 21-year-old. 'The idea was to spend a year in the family business and go for an MBA after that,' he says. But that year changed the way he saw the world. 'During that year, I realized how broken the supply chain was, and that there was no professionalism in the industry. I wanted to build on the concept of legacy, not lineage,' he adds.

After he returned from the University of Warwick in the UK, where he went to study Innovation Entrepreneurship, his dad convinced him to rejoin the family business. He spent the next six years managing yarn procurement, fabric production, and scaling the business and making it sustainable. 'My daily pain point was yarn sourcing, which is extremely middleman-heavy. It was like calling an agent to book your flight tickets back in the old days. Time consuming and redundant,' he says.

For context, India is the largest exporter of cotton in the world and the second-largest exporter of yarn in the world. Textile is the only industry in which India ranks among the top 10 of global market share and 80% of the players consist of small and medium enterprises.

One of the first things Pratik managed to disrupt was the practice of doing every transaction on credit, rather than via advance payments. 'For at least 60 to 120 days, everything is driven on credit in India. We started with a 100% advance payment just before the pandemic and this was the biggest struggle because no one was agreeing to breaking the pre-existing system,' he says.

Keeping that pain point in mind, Yarn Bazaar was born in July 2019. 'So far we've done about ₹350 crore worth of transactions, all in advance payments,' he says. 'I knew people in the diamond industry who explained how trading had gone digital. Now, diamonds are a non-standard, high-value product whereas yarn is a standardized commodity. I thought if diamonds can be done digitally, why not yarn?'

'The USP,' he explains, 'is the quality control, discovery and recommendation that the digital platform provides to the buyer. Typically, between manufacturer and consumer there used to be multiple middlemen; there's a distributer, a dealer, a trader and a broker, and each link is inflating the price for the consumer. To begin with, better prices was our value proposition. The buyer wants good quality with good prices and timely delivery. We wanted to solve for the supply chain problem and the credit problem.'

2020 was the first full year of business for the start-up, and in FY21, Yarn Bazaar managed to do ₹100 crore worth of business, while in FY22, it grew to ₹135 crore. Apart from yarn buying and selling, the company also conducts interviews and podcasts with industry experts, adding value to the sector.

The biggest advantage of being featured on *Shark Tank India*, he says, is that the visibility is very high. Pratik vividly remembers that his episode aired on 5 January. 'Because of the power of OTT and social media, even today people continue to wake up to this new content. Then, they discover Yarn Bazaar and start contacting us. Earlier it was a big effort for us to reach out to buyers and suppliers; now potentially everyone in textiles knows about us,' he says.

The biggest breakthrough on the client front was H&M, which does $7 billion of yarn sourcing globally, wanting to work with him. 'They saw the show and my struggle, and the pain points resonated with them. They wanted us to look at their supply-chain problems and do yarn sourcing for them. That's the power of television,' he says.

Pratik, in fact, was about to drop out of the show as he thought a B2B company would never be able to raise funds. 'I had no confidence that I would make it but I had a conviction when I was starting out. I also had a safety net in my family business. This backstop is important because you can take higher risks. Even if you lose everything, you have something to go back to.'

His pitch, however, impressed the Sharks. He explained, 'We enable textile companies to buy and sell yarn more efficiently through our website or mobile apps, using our proprietary online reverse auction (ORA) process while getting access to flexible unsecured lines of credit. This enables a yarn seller to increase their reach/sales and lead to better margins and lower their credit receivables. At the same time, the yarn buyer can reduce their raw material procurement costs.' This disrupted the processes of procurement, marketing, distribution and sales, which used to be done completely offline via phone calls and one-to-one meetings.

Be shameless

Pratik used to wear his Yarn Bazaar-branded white T-shirts everywhere. 'I would travel by local trains in Mumbai from my house in Malad to my office in Kalbadevi wearing that T-shirt. Many of my fellow passengers who were also from the textile business would come up and ask about my company,' he says. 'It was a great way for me to bring up my company in conversations.'

The amateur rhythm guitarist who used to play in a heavy metal band says that he has never been self-conscious about advertising his company. He would even wear the T-shirt to wedding functions and birthday parties. 'I wanted everyone to know that I'm starting this. This is my brand and I'm going to wear it every freaking time. As an entrepreneur, you have to believe that you're doing something great even if it's nothing. You have to meet people and make them trust your vision. That will only come from self-confidence,' he says. 'One big reason why start-ups fail is because you stop believing in them.'

Pratik believes being shameless is a great tool for a start-up founder. This doesn't mean lacking in dignity, but being unafraid to take bold actions. As an entrepreneur, it is important to be persistent in the face of challenges and setbacks. This often requires stepping out of your comfort zone and taking risks, which may involve being willing to ask for help, seeking funding or promoting ideas to all potential customers or partners.

Pratik's advice is to reach out to founders who have 'been there, done that' without any embarrassment. At least that's what worked for him, he says. 'You've got to be shameless in reaching out to good founders and asking them to share their learnings to quicken your learning curve. I knew if I reach out to 100, 20 out of them would respond and only 10 would actually turn into a meeting. It's like a funnel,' he remarks.

As a result, he has always found encouragement and mentors when he needed them – successful entrepreneurs like Ashish Goyal from EarlySalary, Mohit Sadaani, investor and co-founder (The Mom's Co), and Aaktrit Vaish, co-founder and CEO, Haptik, who guided him when he was starting up. 'I would shamelessly reach out to them,' Pratik reiterates.

Being shameless, he adds, also means being willing to embrace new ideas, even if they are unconventional or unpopular, and to learn from your mistakes. Entrepreneurs often need to be resilient and adaptable, and this means you need to park your ego and be open to feedback and criticism and learning from your experiences. Cultivating shamelessness, which involves putting aside your fears of looking foolish or worrying about what others think of you, is the first step to achieving this.

He feels that being shameless can help entrepreneurs stay focused and be proactive in pursuing opportunities and overcoming obstacles. 'It is an important trait that can help entrepreneurs succeed in a competitive and constantly changing business environment,' he says.

It has helped him in his 'ehsaan se haq tak ka safar' (from depending on favours, to finding success through his own efforts).

Jimmy Shah: The woman with a sweet tooth and a winning idea

What happened when siblings Jash and Pashmi Shah begged their mother Jimmy to make healthy ice-creams? Boom! They ended up with a ₹2.5 crore business that received ₹1 crore from Ashneer Grover, Vineeta Singh and Aman Gupta.

Women entrepreneurs are rare enough. A woman entrepreneur in her fifties is in a special category. When Jimmy appeared on Season 1 of the show along with her son Jash, she charmed the Sharks with her soaring confidence and her passion for her product.

The best businesses, they say, are born when you're able to solve your own life problems through them, and that's exactly what happened with Get-A-Whey. Both Jimmy and her husband were diabetic, but the whole Shah family loved having ice cream. 'There was only one sugar-free ice cream available in the market at that time and that too only in a single, boring vanilla flavour,' Jimmy says. And that's how Get-A-Whey, a premium dessert brand making sugar-free, healthy desserts, was conceived in the kitchen of the Shah family home in Mumbai's Goregaon.

Jimmy, being a great cook (she had made appearances on *Sanjeev Kapoor Ke Kitchen Khiladi* and *Master Chef India* auditions), wanted to solve this problem. At first Jimmy just experimented for the family. 'We did it for ourselves. The ice creams [we made] had five times more protein and were sugar-free,' she says.

Still not thinking of this as a potential business, Jash started casually taking the home-made ice cream for friends at the gym and at work. 'To our surprise, people around me started asking me where to buy this, and eventually we started getting orders,' he says.

Once they understood they were on to something big, the Shahs didn't take much time to kick-start the company with an initial investment of ₹10 lakh put up by family members and a starter team of three, consisting of mum and the two siblings. The growth steadily ramped up.

Get-A-Whey started out by selling a range of sugar-free, low-calorie and protein-rich desserts, such as ice creams and kulfis, across online platforms like Zomato, Swiggy, Swiggy Instamart, Blinkit and its own website. They were hitting around ₹1.5–₹2 lakh worth of orders in just two months. One day, Bollywood actor Ajay Devgn ordered 300 ice cream tubs for everyone on set. 'I thought someone is playing with us to get free ice cream.

I personally went to deliver the ice creams and to check if it really was him,' Jash says.

The word-of-mouth engine in Bollywood went into top gear, and Get-A-Whey became a hot favourite of celebrities like Hrithik Roshan, Karan Johar and Malaika Arora, to name a few. Their order value grew to ₹20 lakh a month. The day Jimmy's episode aired everything was sold out in an hour. Soon after, they were doing ₹40 lakh a month in sales.

Jash's only regret? Not quitting his job sooner to start this. Today, Get-A-Whey is present in 30-plus cities and in more than 150 cloud kitchens.

The maker of sugarless ice creams with added whey protein says the unique X-factor is that all their ice creams are made with real ingredients, are gluten-free and, of course, made with lots of love. The data from the International Diabetes Foundation indicates that one in 11 adult Indians – around seven million in all – has been formally diagnosed with diabetes by 2021, and this number will grow to around 134 million by 2045.[1] So that's a huge slice of the population that could be looking at diabetes-friendly desserts.

According to a report by Smart Research Insights, the yearly consumption of ice cream in India is 400 millilitres per capita.[2] For years, players like Amul, Mother Dairy and Vadilal have been dominating the market,[3] and the market is further expected to grow at a CAGR of 14% between 2021 and 2026 to reach a value of approximately ₹44,200 crore by 2026.[4] 'There's a huge market for us,' Jash says.

In January 2022, Get-A-Whey raised around $2 million (over ₹15 crore) in funding from Sky Gate hospitality, the parent company of Biryani By Kilo. Apart from the financing, Get-A-Whey will now have access to the Biryani By Kilo network of over a hundred cloud kitchens in more than 45 cities. 'These funds will enable us to innovate in terms of product, build an extremely agile distribution and create brand awareness,' the company said in a statement.

The ice cream also retails through modern trade stores in cities like Mumbai, Delhi, Chennai, Bengaluru and Hyderabad. With the investment, Get-A-Whey is expected to become category creators and it also plans to launch new products, such as healthy cakes and vegan ice creams, and to expand into new territories like the Middle East in 2023.

'What we achieved in one year because of the show, we would have taken more than three years to do the same without that push,' Jash says. 'I quit my job the day the episode aired because I started getting so many calls. I felt this is the right time to take the leap of faith.'

While Jash was nervous at first, his mother Jimmy, a serial entrepreneur, motivated everyone to take the plunge.

She had already run a couple of businesses, like a career counselling start-up in the past, and is clearly the risk-taker in the family.

The Shah family feels **a strong sense of ethics is important to becoming an entrepreneur.** 'Business is more about building relationships; it's not just transactional,' Jash says.

In one incident, one of their distributers had an electricity breakdown and ₹7 lakh worth of inventory melted overnight. When the distributer called them to tell Jash about his problem of being out of stock, it was a critical point in his development as an entrepreneur. 'It's not my loss, I felt, but then my mother explained why we should share the loss,' he says.

Jash then shared ₹3.5 lakh worth of the loss. That gesture has reaped a strong relationship. That distributer today takes care of 30% of the company's overall business and he and his family are 'always a phone call away' whenever the Shah family needs them. 'It's all about growing together with your partners and not just being cut-throat or selfish. If you're getting a good night's sleep, you're doing the right thing. I wasn't obligated to help the distributer but businesses are, at the end, all about building long-lasting relationships.'

His ethics, he says, have led the team to multiply from three to 30 in the workforce. **'All successful companies**

know their customers. I know my first 50 customers by name and their birthdays. It was more about understanding what the market wants and where and how you want to play,' he says.

His company received ₹1 crore for a 15% stake from Vineeta, Ashneer and Aman on the show. 'A lot of courage was needed to start the company, quit my job and go on the show with my product. But the validation came with numbers,' he says.

But the company saw its fair share of bad days as well. 'In our first year, I remember 650-plus people saying a straight no to me when I was trying for offline expansion. We had thought retailers would put our products on their shelves because we were getting orders on Instagram, but they did not,' he says. 'That was my breaking point and it made us pivot and start cloud kitchens, and in one month, everything changed.'

He believes that the power of optimism can take you places. He still gets nightmares about the days when he used to travel from Goregaon to Vikroli for a nine-to-five job, come back and work till one in the night and then end the day with extensive research. 'It was essentially two jobs in a day but it paid off in the end.'

Jash now wants to build a company that is globally synonymous with healthy ice cream. 'We want to explore a lot of new categories, like choco lava dessert mix, where you can make it in your own house. Numbers are something that we don't want to chase; we truly want to solve the problem,' he says. Over 60 nutritionists and doctors have already recommended their ice cream. Jash's next target is to hit the ₹100 crore per annum revenue mark. (It hit around ₹35 crore in 2022.)

He says his true learning has been to learn how to be adaptable. The business environment is constantly changing, and entrepreneurs need to be able to respond to these changes to stay competitive. This may involve adapting products or services to meet the changing needs of their customer or adjusting their business model to respond to shifts in the market.

Also, entrepreneurs may face unexpected setbacks, and being adaptable allows them to find creative solutions and pivot their business strategy as needed. 'This can be particularly important in the early stages of a business, when resources are limited and there is a need to be agile and responsive.'

Shows like *Shark Tank*, he feels, educate Indians and help impart important lessons in entrepreneurship. There may be challenges but entrepreneurs like Jimmy and Jash are unfazed. Jimmy often says that she has a vision to turn Get-A-Whey into a billion-dollar company, and that, probably, is how eternal optimists think. With their optimism, resilience and vision, they have more than a fighting chance to achieve their dream!

Gopal Balakrishnan: The art of letting go

There have been 387 pitches in the first two seasons of *Shark Tank India* – far more actually, since there is a screening process before a pitch is cleared to go onscreen. Most of these have failed to impress the Sharks; some of them have been endorsed by one or more of the Sharks and one (which we'll come to later) has been endorsed by all the Sharks. One or two founders have received an offer and bargained for better valuations. Only one, this one, has received an offer and turned it down because the founder had an epiphany and decided instead to focus on family and mental health.

The literal opposite of the phrase 'winners never quit' would be 'losers always quit'. Well, in the world of start-ups, quitters sometimes do win.

Being a winner or being successful is closely tied to being persistent and not giving up, while being a loser is associated with giving up easily. But these rules don't always work in real life. It's simplistic to assume that an entrepreneur's success depends on persistence. But, in fact, it's not advisable to keep trying to do something that is not yielding results. After all, one definition of *insanity is doing the same thing over and over and expecting different results.*

The key is to know the art of letting go. Usually this is referred to **pivoting** in the context of business. The Sharks all speak about the art of learning how to pivot and be flexible. But there is also the art of letting go.

Our next story shows there is no right or wrong decision. Or rather, it's not always possible to say whether a particular decision is 'right' or 'wrong' as it can depend on the context.

For the co-founder of the premium footwear brand Flatheads, Ganesh Balakrishnan, the show was the end of it all. Ganesh had impeccable academic credentials as an alumnus of IIT and IIM. Along with his co-founder Utkarsh Biradar, he had launched a premium casual footwear brand for the urban workforce in 2018.

Their insight: white collar workers were moving from formal to semi-formal to casual dressing in office. While formal pants were being replaced by jeans and joggers, there weren't too many options in the footwear category that had kept pace with this trend – it was either moccasins or sports shoes,

'The only reason we got into it was because we were passionate about shoes. My co-founder had about 150 pairs of shoes and I own about 50,' Ganesh says. Flatheads targeted the casual workwear segment – in fact, the founders had a great pitch for their product, calling it 'T-shirts for your feet'. Slowly, in start-up and VC circles, people started recognizing them for their USP, which was washable and breathable shoes that provided all-day comfort wear.

Ganesh and Utkarsh had been colleagues for a long time. They had earlier established two start-ups together. One of these was Momoe, which was acquired in 2016 by ShopClues, a mobile payments app that allowed users to pay offline merchants like restaurants, grocery stores, electronics, pharmacies, spas, salons, etc.

Since they knew they had a shared passion for shoes, once they conceived Flatheads, the two quit their jobs at ShopClues in April 2018 and started their new business in a few months. Soon they started spending a lot of time with suppliers in India, China, Vietnam, Bangladesh and other countries, trying to understand what goes into making a shoe. This involved working with shoe experts to define and qualify comfort and breathability, and then making a prototype, which took almost a year. Finally, they started producing the product in China, giving the factory an initial order of 3,000 shoes in September 2019. By November 2019, the shoes went on sale on their website.

In 2020, the online brand raised $1 million in a pre-series A round led by the start-up investment platform We Founder Circle and angel network Dexter Angels. The round also witnessed participation from other investors including Gaurav Kapur (TV presenter and founder, Oaktree Sports), Sahil Barua (co-founder, Delhivery) and Radhika Ghai (co-founder, Shopclues).

'The positioning was aspirational for the workforce. We got a lot of entrepreneurs and VCs to wear our shoes, and slowly Flatheads started getting recognized as "great shoes for work",' says Ganesh. But little did they know that a microscopic virus in Wuhan would remove their core selling proposition. Shoes for work suddenly became useless as work from home and Zoom meetings took over.

Flatheads was among the many start-ups devastated by the pandemic. According to a 2021 survey by community platform LocalCircles, about 59% of the start-ups and micro, small and medium enterprises (MSMEs) in India were expected to scale down, shut down or sell themselves off that year due to the impact of the second wave of COVID-19 pandemic.[5] Many start-ups had to reduce their operations or shut down completely due to lockdowns and other restrictions. This led to a catastrophic decline in revenue for many of them.

The pandemic also had an impact on funding and investment for start-ups, as many investors became more cautious and risk-averse due to the uncertain economic environment making it more difficult for start-ups to secure the funding they needed to continue operations and growth. Only a few could find the strength to recover and rebuild in the months to come. Flatheads was one such unfortunate casualty – but only after a desperate struggle.

'We immediately went into survival mode right when the first wave hit. But we kept going. Our network and investors kept telling us that as long as people had feet, they would need shoes. So, fundamentally, the need is not going away. We thought that while we cannot control demand, we should use this time to build our supply.'

They started to contact Indian suppliers who were also suffering because their orders had been cancelled as a result of export demand being hit. They started manufacturing in the Tiruppur-Coimbatore belt in Tamil Nadu, while assembly was done in Jalandhar and Kanpur. By their next set of orders of 5,000 shoes in August 2020, they were a completely made-in-India brand.

But the second wave hit just as demand had got going again. 'We had to keep the morale of the team high. A lot of them lost faith; it was very demotivating for them and there was a lot of attrition. At every stage, we asked ourselves – are we growing enough? The market is going away so what should we do? Should we even position ourselves as shoes for work?'

It's not like they didn't try to pivot. Ganesh and team started focusing on comfort rather than calling them 'shoes for work'. Soon they started selling on other channels like Cred and Amazon, they even went international with Zappos, the largest marketplace for shoes in the US.

The marketing focus and the momentum shifted to 'for comfort' shoes made for both men and women (earlier they had only focused on men); they invested in new designs and marketing, and they even got a brand ambassador. But as their third order of 10,000 shoes was underway, the third wave of the pandemic 'broke their back'.

'We ran out of money and by the time I went on the show, we were already at a point where we would shut if we didn't get the funding,' Ganesh says. While Aman advised him to take a step back and do something else, Vineeta and Peyush came up with an offer for 33% equity. But by then, Ganesh and Utkarsh had decided that they both needed to step back and wind up Flatheads because they didn't want to cope with that level of stress, and they wanted more family-time.

'Entrepreneurship is a hard journey but maybe national television was not the best moment for me to break down, relook at my life and decide to shut down the company. My co-founder, too, decided he no longer wanted to stay because he didn't have the financial muscle to continue.'

Ganesh described his thought processes: 'Vineeta Singh asked, what would I do if I got the money. That got me thinking and then Aman Gupta spoke about being in a similar situation, and how he took a two-year break to clear his mind. During that time, I started thinking about my journey and the impact it had on my family, which made me emotional.'

Quitting can be a difficult decision, but it can also be a valuable learning experience. Sometimes we realize that something isn't right for us, and it's important to accept that. Quitting can be a way to allow ourselves the freedom to pursue other opportunities. It's also important to prioritize your well-being. And that's exactly what Ganesh did on the show.

Quitting something can feel like a failure, but it's important to recognize that it can also be a form of self-improvement. 'After being in survival mode for three years, one big lesson was to pay attention to my health – physical and mental. One needs to first stay alive to try and make another start-up happen,' says Ganesh about that difficult decision.

It involved a lot of introspection.

'We would have done better had the pandemic not been there. But fundamentally would it have been successful? I have no idea. Would the brand still be alive? I have no idea. It's very easy to blame external circumstances but you get a lot of perspective when you take a step back,' he observes. 'There was a clear end to the thing because we were out of money and we couldn't raise additional funding.'

WHEN IS IT TIME TO QUIT?

While it can be difficult for a start-up founder to know when it's time to quit, there are a few signs that it might be time to consider moving on:

- **Lack of progress:** If the start-up is not making progress towards its goals, it might be time to re-evaluate the plan and consider whether it's worth continuing.
- **Running out of resources:** If you are running out of financial resources or the team is stretched too thin, it might be necessary to consider quitting.
- **Loss of passion:** Starting a business can be a demanding and time-consuming process, and it's important for the founder to be passionate about the product or service they are offering. If the passion is gone, it might be time to move on.
- **Personal circumstances:** Sometimes, one's personal circumstances can make it necessary to quit the start-up. For example, if the founder is facing a major life change, such as starting a family or moving to a new location, it might be necessary to put the start-up on hold or consider quitting.

According to Ganesh, some people want to make a profitable business, and others might want to make a growth business. 'For us the goal was growth. We had reached 30% to 35% of that growth. If we had reached 75% to 80%, we could have continued after two years. You evaluate that it's a good time to go,' he says.

Another very important aspect was the emotional component. 'We were not getting repeat customers and even the ones that were sold, we didn't get to know whether they were working or not. There was uncertainty; we had already lost half our team. **You don't get time to spend with your 10-year-old daughter. Your wife is supporting the family and has been the breadwinner for the last 10 years. There's only so much emotional stress you can take,**' he says.

'But as an entrepreneur, the baby never dies in your mind. The thought crosses my mind multiple times that I could have pushed harder,' he confesses.

Mental health is seldom talked about in work environments, including start-ups. Talking about mental health can be intimidating for many, as it requires vulnerability and openness. This can be especially difficult in a start-up environment where there may be pressure to project strength and resilience. 'I have gone and sought therapy. It's not just about feeling high all the time. You can spiral into depression very quickly,' he says. 'I don't think I'll ever get over it.'

Even now, Ganesh talks about building a financial corpus for at least five years before thinking about building a start-up again. For a well-networked IIT–IIM graduate like him, getting back into the workforce was not a challenge. 'A pedigree like that gives you the luxury of getting plum jobs right out of college and by the time you're 40, you have enough money saved up and you can think of doing something that really excites you and take that entrepreneurial plunge. Otherwise, most people who are not from that pedigree will join salaried jobs and build their financial prowess slowly,' he says.

But as they say, in every failure there's a lesson to be learnt. His first and foremost lesson was the importance of being nimble. 'In a pandemic, when nobody was buying any shoes, we got very nervous about building anything new. Maybe if I would have started making chappals sooner, I would have sold them a lot more, or had we pivoted to quickly going international where lockdowns were not so stringent, I would have sold a lot more shoes, or changing the concept from work shoe to completely going into active lifestyle could have helped. A lot of these questions are still unanswered.'

He also feels having the right type of financial investor could potentially have helped them survive the downturn. 'A lot of the money that we had raised was through our personal networks. When the future became uncertain, they would not have invested again. Had we raised cash through an institutional investor, maybe things would have been different.'

For Ganesh, one of the biggest learnings was to focus on his health. **'When I went through therapy, I realized I should have done this sooner. Don't postpone it; recognize the signs of it early,'** he says.

Every entrepreneur has had multiple moments like these. Everybody goes through that survival moment.

You can kill off the business but somewhere, the entrepreneur in you never dies.

'I have some two hundred shoes left on my website. Two or three people still come and buy them every week.'

The Sharks think Ganesh will be back in business soon, maybe launching another start-up. 'We've all been in Ganesh's shoes at some point in our business and that is why his story resonated with all of us so well and made us almost teary-eyed. We could all remember and relive the time when we wanted to quit and do something else, when our runway was about to get over,' Vineeta says.

Anuja and Ravi Kabra: Hitting refresh

Anuja and Ravi Kabra had a good life in Australia – they had spent years establishing themselves in the new country and even bought a house. But when Ravi's father was diagnosed with oral cancer, Ravi decided to return to India and hit refresh.

Ravi says that if a person with an entrepreneurial mindset wants to start something, the idea will come by itself. This is probably what happened when Ravi's sister was visiting them from India when the Kabras were in Sydney. She had bought some local brand of ice popsicle tubes and was packing them in a suitcase. When quizzed about why she was taking so many with her, she simply said that there was no brand of ice popsicles in India that she could trust. 'That was my Eureka moment!' he recalls.

He thought to himself that India is a big market with a hot and humid climate where ice popsicles would sell like hot cakes (or, indeed, like ice popsicles!) 'Our gut feeling said that's the gap in the market we need to fill.'

Soon after that, the Hyderabad-based couple launched what the duo claims to be India's first ice popsicle brand – Skippi – that made an appearance in Season 1 of the show. Both of them had over a decade of experience of managing their family business of import-export and distribution, and they also had years of experience in the food and beverage (F&B) space with multinational brands like Krispy Kreme and George Weston foods.

Before starting Skippi, the duo had flirted with seven to eight ideas but some had issues such as requiring high investment or not having enough market size, while others were not emotionally exciting. **'You have to go with your gut feeling. It has to be a balance of something that excites you with a little bit of market evaluation. People rely too much on market analysis and research and fail to understand that passion and excitement needs to be there for an entrepreneur to get into something,'** Ravi observes.

For an entrepreneur, drive is very important, while primary market research helps you understand whether there's a demand for it. 'We started giving samples to people and they kept asking us where to buy it. That meant it was the right product and we became confident that there's demand for it,' he adds.

But ice popsicles was not their first idea. It actually started with alcohol-based ice-pops that young people would really enjoy. When Ravi and Anuja started doing their market research, they realized that in India, every state has legal limitations in terms of alcohol and compliances. 'I thought that would become a distribution nightmare for me. Because I wanted to do something that was easily acceptable at a mass level and scale it up from there.'

A skilled entrepreneur knows how important it is to be able to adapt quickly and be flexible. It's a skill that helps them succeed in a rapidly changing business environment. That's because start-up founders often come across new challenges and the ability to quickly adapt and find creative solutions can be critical to the success of their ventures and to stay relevant for much longer.

Ravi has had prior experience in running a start-up that was similar to Justdial, and he put all his learnings to good use while starting-up this time. **'I learnt that we were trying to scale up too fast and we did not have a USP. That's where we failed.** Sometimes people try to be too careful and have checkboxes for everything, which doesn't help. They start-up only when they have a job and know they have something to go back to – it doesn't work like that in real life. **If you've done your market research and are confident, you have to take the leap of faith.** Whether you sink or swim, that's your destiny, but you're never going to know unless you give your 100%.'

Post *Shark Tank*, people have treated the Kabras like celebrities. 'They believe it's been very easy. But the kind of stress and pressure Anuja and I take every day is humongous.'

Anuja, being a mother of two kids, has to manage the house as well as the business. **'I've totally come to understand that while building this brand I will probably not be as connected to my kids like I was in Australia. You have to live with it, and people don't often talk about this dark side,'** she says.

Exposure on TV will give you attention – but sometimes the business may not be ready for it. 'Had I not been on national TV, we would have been growing under the radar, which would have given us a way of strategically growing month-on-month gradually. But with us coming on TV, we became the talk of the town, and when you come from that kind of popularity, scaling up and keeping up the customer's experience becomes a big challenge'.

'We were used to doing 30 to 35 orders a day, and suddenly we were receiving 3,500 orders. This is a problem not many can tackle. We had to build up capacity instantly. We recruited people who were walking on the road. **Today, Indian consumers are so spoilt, they believe everyone is Amazon. We did not have that kind of network or infrastructure in place, unfortunately.**'

But it helped that he had his partner to share the pleasures and pain with. 'It was easy in the sense that we knew each other for 15 years before working together. Sometimes, work–life balance goes for a toss and but it's a 24-hour work day in a start-up,' Ravi says. 'Having a good co-founder is a must, Anuja and I keep pushing each other when we're low. We would have given up long back if we did not have each other.'

According to Ravi, a lot of start-ups would not have been able to sustain this kind of attention and demand. 'We were manufacturing only 2,500 litres a day. In a span of four months, from January to April 2022, we scaled it up to nearly six times to 12,000 litres per day, and for that, I would like to give some credit to the both of us,' he says.

When they were not able to deliver at Amazon-Prime speeds, they also faced complaints that they were fake and it had been a mistake ordering from them. 'I remember when the entire world was celebrating 31 December, we had crashed. We were so tired of constantly handling that kind of a pressure.'

He says that for a start-up founder 'selfless perseverance' is key, and they must be passionately attached to the idea of the business. **'That will drive you in the first place. If you're bored, you'll give up very soon.'** There are a lot of times, he thinks, when you believe it's time to stop because something's not working out. 'Right then you need to think about the entire project altogether, or make some changes.'

Skippi was the only brand in Season 1 where all six Sharks invested a total of ₹1.2 crore. 'Pre-*Shark Tank*, we were at about ₹5 lakh a month; post the show we touched about ₹2 crore a month,' says Ravi.

The Sharks, he adds, have identified the kind of start-ups which need more of their time, and the ones which need less. 'They're helping not by giving time, but by giving us very strategic viewpoints in terms of where we should head next and, also, the plethora of contacts like investors, manufacturing consultants, collaborators, etc., which come automatically because of their experience in the industry.'

The duo is all set for its next leg of expansion. Earlier, they weren't exporting, but Skippi is now available in Canada, New Zealand, Uganda, Nepal, Singapore, Dubai, etc. In India, they've already reached 8,000 pincodes in 22 states and they get orders from unusual places like Jammu and Kashmir, Andaman and Nicobar, and Nagaland.

One of the things that helped them scale up quickly was the fact that they had 70% offline and 30% online business expansions which reverses the ratio that new-age start-up founders prefer to follow.

Knowing their strengths in distribution and manufacturing, they targeted the tougher offline market first. 'We have to put in more efforts in increasing our online base as well. Most start-ups do it the other way around but our decades of experience in the F&B space has taught us that the largest companies like Parle and Marico became big on the basis of their distribution network by building physical presence first,' he says.

The Kabras started by investing ₹55 lakh of their own money. Skippi today has grown 40% since then. Now that's a sweet story.

Conclusions

Making it

Are you ready to start? Hopefully this book has given you a sense of what the Sharks look for before they consider a business or its founders investment-worthy. They want optimism, empathy, passion and flexibility. There have been 387 pitches onscreen, several thousand pitches that didn't make it onto the show and only 170 deals along with another 40 offers that did not result in deals. That should give you a sense of how difficult it is to raise seed funding for a business.

There are a few other points that the Sharks didn't directly address in much detail but which are worth noting.

One is that angel investors prefer businesses launched by co-founders. Two heads are really better than one – even if that one is a genius. People have complementary skills and every successful business needs those. A brilliant inventor may have no head for double-entry accounting or how to brand and market a product.

Take Apple, for example. There were two faces to the company when they operated out of a garage and launched the first revolutionary Mac personal computer back in the 1980s. Steve Jobs was the charismatic frontman who did the branding and the pitching, and worked out the marketing ideas. Steve Wozniak was the crazy-smart engineer, who actually designed the devices and made sure they worked as advertised.

One of the Sharks, Aman, explained why he and his co-founder Sameer work well together. In Get-A-Whey, diabetic mom Jimmy put the recipes together and provides advice on the ethics, while her son and daughter do the marketing.

Another thing the Sharks consider very carefully is the product-market fit. This is more of an art than a science, but it's very important. The product-market fit refers to the degree to which a product or service meets the needs of a specific market, and we've described it in more detail in the introduction.

If you see that your business isn't doing as well as you thought it would, be ready to pivot. It's good for an entrepreneur to be persistent and keep going even if there are setbacks. But don't be afraid to change your product or redefine your service or even look for a different target market. Most of the Sharks have pivoted, not just once but a few times. Even small tweaks can make a big difference in finding the right product-market fit.

Be prepared for disappointments and also weigh the

costs and benefits carefully before taking the plunge into business. Starting a business is challenging, and win or lose, it requires significant sacrifices and changes in lifestyle.

A start-up founder should be prepared for the following:

1. **It's 24x7:** A start-up requires time and hard work. Founders have to put in long hours. This means sacrificing time with family and friends, as well as putting aside personal hobbies and interests.
2. **Your finances are going to yo-yo**: Starting a business is financially risky, and founders may have to invest their own money or take loans. This means sacrificing financial stability and security. Be prepared to live on very little – Vineeta Singh turned down a ₹1 crore job offer to live on ₹10,000 a month.
3. **Your personal comfort**: Forget about it! You'll have to deal with uncertainty, long hours and making difficult decisions.
4. **You might fail**: Many businesses fail. Be prepared to lose it all and start again from scratch. Even the Sharks' life stories indicate this – many of them failed at a couple of ventures before they made it.

At least a couple of the Sharks also talked about the need to maintain mental health and emotional stability.

Vineeta cries when she's overwrought and finds it a great outlet for her emotions. Namita meditates regularly. Ganesh Balakrishnan, who decided to shut down his business, spoke about going to therapy and wished he had done it earlier. Being an entrepreneur is stressful for sure. The Kabras are clear that without each other they wouldn't be able to handle the pressures of running Skippi.

The highs have to be really high to compensate for all the probable stress and hardship. You can't launch a business simply because you want to get rich. Founders who make it are the ones who actively enjoy running their businesses, and for most of them wealth creation isn't necessarily their primary concern.

The investment legend Warren Buffett says, 'In the world of business the people who are most successful are those who are doing what they love.'

So find a business idea, do all the research you need, make sure there's a 'founder-product fit', and slog it out – but above all, remember, as a founder, you have to love what you're doing.

Good luck!

Notes

1. Vineeta Singh's Secret to Sweet Success

1. Harsh Upadhyay, 'SUGAR Cosmetics Closes $50 Mn Series D Round', Entracker, 31 May 2022. https://entrackr.com/2022/05/sugar-cosmetics-closes-50-mn-series-d-round/.
2. Kadambari Rana, 'Why Educating Women Is More Important than We Realize', *The Times of India*, 27 September 2022. https://www.unesco.org/en/articles/why-educating-women-more-important-we-realize.
3. Ibid.
4. 'SUGAR Cosmetics on Picking Up Majority Stake in ENN Beauty', ET Retail.com, 31 January 2022. https://retail.economictimes.indiatimes.com/news/health-and-beauty/cosmetics-and-fragrances/sugar-cosmetics-on-picking-up-majority-stake-in-enn-beauty/89234656.
5. David J. Schwartz, *The Magic of Thinking Big,* Touchstone, 1987.

2. Aman Gupta and His Three BFs: Be Fast, Fearless and Frugal

1. 'Shark Tank India's Aman Gupta impressed by kid who names him, his company in answer sheet: 'Petition to make this change…', *The Indian Express*, 2 February 2023. https://indianexpress.com/article/entertainment/television/shark-tank-india-aman-gupta-impressed-by-kid-who-named-him-company-boat-answer-sheet-8419348/.
2. 'India's #1 Earwear Audio brand as per IDC', boAt-lifestyle.com. https://www.boat-lifestyle.com/blogs/news/indias-1-earwear-audio-brand-as-per-idc.
3. Harsh Upadhyay and Md. Salman Ashrafi, 'boAt Posts Rs 2,873 Cr Revenue in FY22, Profit Dips 20%', Entracker, 19 January 2023. https://entrackr.com/2023/01/boat-posts-rs-2873-cr-revenue-in-fy22-profit-dips-20/#:~:text=With%20over%202.3X%20jump,month%20period%20ending%20March%202022.
4. Pranav Mukul and Digbijay Mishra, 'Boat closes $60-million funding from Warburg and Malabar Investments', *The Economic Times*, 28 October 2022. https://economictimes.indiatimes.com/tech/funding/boat-closes-60-million-financing-through-convertible-notes-postpones-ipo/articleshow/95127978.cms?from=mdr.
5. Harsh Upadhyay and Md. Salman Ashrafi, 'boAt Posts Rs 2,873 Cr Revenue in FY22, Profit Dips 20%', Entracker, 19 January 2023. https://entrackr.com/2023/01/boat-posts-rs-2873-cr-revenue-in-fy22-profit-dips-20/#:~:text=With%20over%202.3X%20jump,month%20period%20ending%20March%202022.

6. Ibid.
7. NDM News Network, 'Imagine Marketing (boAt) Ranks 2nd in Global Wearable Market', Digital Terminal, 29 December 2022. https://digitalterminal.in/news/imagine-marketing-boat-ranks-2nd-in-global-wearable-market/31975.html#:~:text=Imagine%20Marketing%2C%20the%20parent%20company,Quarterly%20Wearable%20Device%20Tracker%20Q3CY2022.

3. Why Peyush Bansal Thinks Empathy Is His Secret Weapon

1. 'Build Query: Funding Rounds', Crunchbase. https://www.crunchbase.com/search/funding_rounds/field/organizations/last_funding_type/lenskart-com.
2. Team Inc42, 'Decoding Angel Funding for Indian Startups', Inc42, 28 March 2022. https://inc42.com/resources/decoding-angel-funding-for-indian-startups/.

4. Namita Thapar's Success Mantra

1. Namita Thapar, *The Dolphin and the Shark: Stories on Entrepreneurship*, Penguin Random House, 2022.
2. Ibid.
3. Ibid.
4. Dia Rekhi, 'Only 1.5% of Total Funding Goes to Indian Startups With Women Founders', *The Economic Times*, 14 June 2022. https://economictimes.indiatimes.com/

tech/startups/only-1-5-of-total-funding-goes-to-indian-startups-with-women-founders/articleshow/92209557.cms?from=mdr.

5. From Steve Jobs' commencement address at Stanford University, 2005. '"You've Got to Find What You Love," Jobs Says', Stanford News, 12 June 2005. https://news.stanford.edu/2005/06/12/youve-got-find-love-jobs-says/.
6. Namita Thapar, *The Dolphin and the Shark: Stories on Entrepreneurship*, Penguin Random House, 2022.

6. Fail Fast, Learn Faster Like Amit Jain

1. Manish Singh, 'India's CarDekho Becomes Unicorn with $250 Million Fundraise', Techcrunch, 13 October 2021. https://techcrunch.com/2021/10/12/cardekho-becomes-unicorn-with-250-million-fundraise/.
2. 'CarDekho Group's FY22 Consolidated Operating Revenue Grows by 81 Per Cent to Rs 1,600 Crores', cardekho.com, 3 January 2023. https://www.cardekho.com/india-car-news/cardekho-groups-fy22-consolidated-operating-revenue-grows-by-81-per-cent-to-rs-1600-crores-30184.htm.
3. Harsh Upadhyay and Md. Salman Ashrafi, 'CarDekho's Scale Nears Rs 1,600 Cr in FY22, Used Cars Form 50% Income', Entracker, 5 January 2023. https://entrackr.com/2023/01/cardekhos-scale-nears-rs-1600-cr-in-fy22-used-cars-form-50-income/.

7. Lessons from *Shark Tank India*

1. Preetu Nair, 'By 2045, India Will Have 134.3 Mn People

With Diabetes', *The Times of India*, 8 December 2017. https://timesofindia.indiatimes.com/city/kochi/by-2045india-will-have-134-3-mn-people-with-diabetes/articleshow/61975596.cms.

2. 'India Ice Cream Market Study 2019', marketresearch.com, September 2019. https://www.marketresearch.com/Smart-Research-Insights-v3920/India-Ice-Cream-Study-12642594/.
3. Bhavya Kaushal, 'Started in Their Mother's Kitchen, This Sibling Duo's Brand Is Making a Mark with Premium Protein Ice Cream', YourStory, 10 March 2021. https://yourstory.com/smbstory/get-a-whey-mumbai-protein-ice-cream-brand.
4. Expert Market Research, 'India Ice Cream Market Outlook'. https://www.expertmarketresearch.com/reports/india-ice-cream-market.
5. 'Impact of COVID 2nd Wave: 59% Startups and MSMEs in India Likely to Scale Down, Shut Down or Sell Themselves This Year', LocalCircles, 27 May 2021. https://www.localcircles.com/a/press/page/covid-small-business-survey#.Y7rBn3ZBxPZ.

A Note on the Author and Co-author

Shark Tank India is the hit Indian Hindi-language business reality television series that airs on Sony Entertainment Television. The show is the Indian franchise of the American show *Shark Tank*. It shows entrepreneurs making business presentations to a panel of investors, or Sharks, who decide whether to invest in their company.

Meet Prerna Lidhoo, an accomplished journalist with a skill for telling stories through both the written word and on-camera reporting. With over eight years of experience under her belt, Lidhoo has developed a reputation as a reporter with a knack for bringing complex issues to life using engaging storytelling tools. At organizations like *Hindustan Times*, *Fortune India*, *India Today* and others, she has interviewed a wide range of personalities from the world of business, start-ups, media and entertainment. Her passion for the written word is matched only by her love for reading and watching world cinema.

To download the app scan the QR Code with a QR scanner app